MYSTERY FANCIER

March·April 1983
Vol.7 · No.2

$2.50

The Mystery Fancier

Volume 7, Number 2
March/April 1983

TABLE OF CONTENTS

MYSTERIOUSLY SPEAKING	Page 1
Young Detective Kildare, by Evelyn Herzog	Page 2
The World of Nero Wolfe, by Asbjorn Skytte (Translated by E.F. Bleiler)	Page 11
An Interview with Desmond Bagley, by Jane S. Bakerman	Page 13
Deduction in Duplicate, by Alan S. Mosier	Page 19
IT'S ABOUT CRIME: by Marvin Lachman	Page 22
REEL MURDERS: Movie Reviews by Walter Albert	Page 27
VERDICTS: Book Reviews	Page 31
THE DOCUMENTS IN THE CASE: Letters	Page 40

The Mystery Fancier
(USPS:428-590)
is edited and published bi-monthly by
Guy M. Townsend
1711 Clifty Drive
Madison, IN 47250

SUBSCRIPTION RATES: Second-class mail, U.S. and Canada, $12.00 per year (6 issues); first-class mail, U.S. and Canada, $15.00; overseas surface mail, $12.00; overseas air mail, $18.00. Overseas subscribers please pay in international money order, check drawn on U.S. bank, or currency; no checks drawn on foreign banks, please.

Single copy price: $2.50

Second-class postage paid at Madison, Indiana

Copyright 1982 by Guy M. Townsend
All rights reserved for contributors
ISSN:0146-3160

Jud Sapp is dead. Unless you happen to be a devout fan of Rex Stout, or a student who passed through the Atlanta elementary school of which he was the principal, chances are this won't mean much to you. People die every day—every second—the good along with the bad, and if we mourned the death of every good man we'd never get any living done ourselves. So we tend, when we hear of the death of someone not close to us, to shake our heads, mutter something like "That's too bad," and then go along with our lives as though nothing had happened. I don't want that to happen with Jud. I want you people to know that goodness in this world diminished considerably when he died.

When I first heard that Jud was terminally ill with cancer I wanted to curse and I wanted to cry. I did a little of both. Jud was just in his early forties and was as full of the joy of living as anyone I have ever known. He was a good, decent, generous, honest, and gentle man. I first met him through our shared interest in Nero Wolfe. It was in the mid-seventies, and I had just begun work on what was to become the nineteen-part "Nero Wolfe Saga" which ran in these pages for three years. From the way Jud acted, you would have thought that I was doing all that work just for him; he thanked me repeatedly and profusely and said that he would be forever in my debt. If that sounds phony to you, it's just because you didn't know Jud; he was that kind of guy.

I only got to see Jud twice. The first time was in 1977, when the Southern Historical Association met in Atlanta. I let Jud know I would be in town and suggested that we get together. He countered by suggesting that I stay at his home, but, as he had never met me before and I am reluctant to inflict myself on people who are not already aware of what they are getting into, I declined with thanks. Nevertheless he insisted on taking me out to eat the first night and then having me over to his home for dinner the second night. He and his wife, Linda, produced as magnificent a meal as I have ever had in a private home, and the memory of those two evenings of warm and friendly companionship will live in my mind forever.

I returned to Atlanta for an interview the next year, and, Jud and Linda having renewed their offer to put me up, I stayed with them overnight. With typical generosity, Jud put himself and his automobile at my disposal, meeting my flight at the airport, which was many miles from the remote suburb in which he lived, driving me to my appointment downtown the next day and then coming back to get me afterward, and finally making that long journey to the airport once again to deliver me to my flight. And all the time he made me feel

[Continued on page 10]

Young Detective Kildare

Evelyn Herzog

> Not a detective? Confound you, make yourself into one, then! A doctor has to be a nurse, a cook, a family lawyer, a mother, a father, a rat-killer, and why in the name of God can't he go a step backward, or forward, and be a detective?
>
> —Leonard Gillespie

The first thing you ought to understand about the Dr. Kildare stories written by Frederick Faust (as Max Brand) in conjunction with the Lew Ayres/Lionel Barrymore MGM movie series in the thirties and the forties is that they're rather hokey. Time after time in these short books everything depends on Jimmy Kildare's ability and character--his patient's life and/or sanity, his own professional career and often that of a colleague, his parents' hopes for him, his future with the woman he loves, old Gillespie's desire for a worthy successor to his diagnostic expertise, everything that makes Kildare's life worth living. Invariably Kildare, having been put into an impossible situation, is offered a way—at the expense of his own conscience--of satisfying the world's demands and saving all he loves, and invariably he turns it down. Yet with equal regularity the right somehow prevails: Kildare, with his uncompromising honesty, accomplishes all that is required of him and more besides, and in the end we learn that the expedient solution would have ruined everything while costing Kildare his self-respect.

Yet for some readers, myself included, these stories continue to be a source of great enjoyment, partly because of just this simplified and romantic scheme of life, and partly for the classic figures of Gillespie and Kildare, the cranky old wizard and his idealistic acolyte. Still another part of the appeal of the Kildare stories and movies lies in the elements of mystery and detection that figure in them. These are, of course, subsidiary to the medical theme, but here and there throughout his career Kildare does do some classic detective work (however amateurish), and this is the subject of my remarks.

The novels and stories I have in mind are **Young Doctor Kildare, Calling Dr. Kildare, The Secret of Dr. Kildare,** "Dr. Kildare's Search," **Dr. Kildare Takes Charge, Dr. Kildare's Crisis, Dr. Kildare's Trial,** and "Dr. Kildare's Hardest Case."[1] There have been other stories about a Dr. Kildare and a Dr. Gillespie, but they are distinctly different incarnations of the characters and do not form a consistent whole with these eight tales.

WARNING: I will be discussing details of the plots and unconcernedly giving away endings. Since the Kildare stories are a far cry from fair-play mysteries, however, I don't think this is likely to impair anyone's enjoyment of them.

One of the first things we learn about **Young Dr. Kildare** is that he has at least a technical flair for medical observation and deduction. When he visits home, we see his parents through his eyes and are presented with analyses of their medical conditions. Though he's with them, his attention keeps going back to the details of an unexplained fever case--not out of compassion (he doesn't even know the patient's name!) but from intellectual curiosity--until he finally comes up with the correct diagnosis, wires the information back to the doctor in charge, and dismisses the matter from his mind. There's something acute but cold about this young Jimmy Kildare.

Virtually his first action as a new intern in New York is the diagnosis that will change his life. The hospital's Grand Old Man, Dr. Leonard Gillespie, is a renowned, idiosyncratic, and aging diagnostician who has for years been searching for a young doctor to train as his successor. The current crop of interns is duly paraded before him. In a sort of ghastly parallel to Cinderella and the glass slipper, Kildare is revealed as the one for whom Gillespie has searched, by diagnosing almost at a glance what Gillespie alone already knows--that the older doctor is dying of cancer. On this introduction is built the stories' central theme, that of Kildare's apprenticeship to Gillespie--a relationship sometimes warmly supportive, sometimes knock-down-drag-out in nature.

Their course does not run smooth. Almost at once Kildare gets into a peck of trouble and has to turn detective to extricate himself. On an ambulance run he has revived an attempted suicide named Barbara Chanler. After her admission to the hospital, he continues to spend a good deal of time at her bedside, trying to solve the vexing puzzle of why a rich and healthy young woman would try to gas herself. He wins her confidence, but only up to a point. She is deeply mortified by some action in her past, something too shameful to live with. She cannot be prevailed upon to reveal her secret to her family or fiance, not even to Kildare, though she speaks most freely with him. The hospital confines her to the psychopathic ward, the family calls in a noted psychiatrist, and all concerned expect Kildare to come across with a complete report of what Ms. Chanler has told him about herself.

But she has sworn him to secrecy, and he is determined to keep his promise. Medical ethics, as well, require that he do so--or, rather, they would so require if she were sane. He is not expected to respect the confidences of an irrational person, and, since this is how the medical authorities (except for Kildare) regard her, they pressure him to talk. The only way out, for him and for her, is for Kildare to prove Barbara Chanler sane by establishing the antecedents of her suicide attempt and relieving her fears about herself.

Soon, though, thanks to other acts of insubordination, Kildare can see that he's finished at the hospital at any event; but, since his patient's mind and life may still be salvageable even if his career is not, he perseveres on her behalf. Gillespie sets him on the trail by passing on the information that, not long before the suicide attempt, she had begun acting strangely after a late-night party. An encounter with a clinic patient gives Kildare a clue to the source of the befuddlement Ms. Chanler had displayed at that time. Kildare gets the names of others at the party by somewhat devious inquiry and tracks down Stewart Walden, the man with whom his patient had last been seen that night. By means of a poor but nonetheless effective impersonation of a narcotics cop, he gets Walden to tell all.

"All" turns out to consist of an inexperienced young woman with too much to drink and her first use of marijuana, a companion with an eye to the main chance, a dazed visit to a shady nightclub, a blackout, and an awakening in a strange bed with no idea what's been going on but a vivid imagination. As it happened, though, Barbara Chanler's collapse had been so emphatic that Walden had lost all interest in everything but keeping her alive. So, despite her fears, she can be told that her virtue has survived the escapade intact. For her there is to be no more shrinking from her respectable family, no more suicide attempts, no more fears of some sort of morbid immorality. As for Kildare, he is off the hook with the hospital authorities, not only over his handling of the Chanler case but for all his other infractions, thanks to some brisk behind-the-scenes work by Gillespie.

While the solution of this case hardly puts Kildare up there in the same league with Sherlock Holmes, it's evidently more than most of his fellow interns could have managed. Along the way, Kildare displays a few of the distinguishing characteristics of the classic detective.

With all the dispassion of Holmes himself, he fails to notice that his patient is an extraordinarily beautiful young woman until it is emphatically pointed out to him. In fact, Kildare at this stage tends very much to see only problems, not people. This is a good trait, in that he can't be distracted when he's on a case, but it's a failing in a man who aspires to be a superb diagnostician and who must not be blind to the full humanity of his patients. In the future, Gillespie will arrange to loosen him up a bit.

Kildare shows an ability to make non-medical deductions from physical clues--"She was educated abroad, rides horses and plays tennis," he remarks of Ms. Chanler on the basis of a hurried physical examination and an overheard exclamation.

His manner, again like Holmes, is such that patients are moved to take him into their confidence. One nurse, observing what she takes to be his lack of scruple in charming information out of his vulnerable patient, icily remarks to him, "Like peeping through a keyhole, isn't it? . . . What a detective you would have made! What a **friendly** detective!"

Again, for the diagnostician as for the consulting detective, an encyclopedic knowledge of precedents is vital. Holmes once remarked that "there is a strong family resemblance about misdeeds, and if you have all the details of a thousand at your finger ends, it is odd if you can't unravel the thousand and first." KIldare sees the necessity of his acquiring a comparable knowledge of medical precedents. He says, "I know what I want. A big hospital like that one. Where the sick come by thousandas and thousands, every disease under the sun and you see and keep on seeing in such numbers that at last you know the face of it."

That's what he wants, and that's what he gets. At the beginning of **Calling Dr. Kildare**, though, the intern has made a major tactical error in the pursuit of this education. He's convinced himself that the mere dogged accumulation of facts will turn him into a diagnostician. Insight and human understanding are not on his agenda. He continues to meet only symptoms, not people. Gillespie, who knows that only the lessons learned "with time and pain, with the help of God and the power of prayer more than I ever had help from book and microscopes," are of any value, and whose illness gives him no time to wait for Kildare to grow out of the bookworm phase, decides on a drastic course of treatment for his protege. He fires Kildare, gets him assigned to outpatient service where he can see a bit more of life, and pushes women into his path (or, more precisely, one woman, Nurse Mary Lamont). But the old man has outfoxed himself. Kildare falls in love, all right, but with distinctly the wrong woman. And Kildare starts getting involved with people, but mostly with a likeable young low-life named Nick who is suffering from an unreported gunshot wound, requiring a clandestine operation, an equally illegal transfusion, shelter from arrest on a murder charge, and the ministrations of an intern who's absent without official leave from the hospital. The flouting of hospital rules is bad enough, but by not reporting the murder suspect and his gunshot wound Kildare has put himself in trouble with the law. When Nick is nabbed by the cop on the beat, it seems certain that he and Kildare will sink together.

And yet, if only Nick were innocent of murder, strings might be pulled and exceptions made for his Good Samaritan. Kildare sets out to solve the murder, and, though it doesn't turn out to be a very taxing investigation, at least he beats the police to the solution. Nick has told him that he had a grudge against the dead man, Bowler Smith, because Smith had reportedly bad-mouthed Nick's sister Rosalie (who is, incidentally, the woman Kildare has fallen for). Nick had followed Smith with the iintention of starting a fracas, but before he could do so a third man stepped up and shot them both. Kildare perceptively asks for the name of the "friend" who had originally told Nick about Smith's insult and thereby started the feud. The man is one "Happy" Leeman. Kildare finds him and confronts him with his theory that Leeman had a grudge of his own against Smith and had set Nick up to take the blame for Smith's death in a gunfight intended to be fatal to both men. Kildare's passion for facts without close attention to situations almost gets his neck broken, for he has visited Leeman unarmed, but a strong-arm friend providentially backs him up. (In this failing Kildare has something of a precedent in Holmes, who confessed himself "absent-minded" in the matter of self-protection.) Kildare finds the automatic which both killed Smith and wounded Nick, Leeman is carted off to jail, and Nick is released.

Gillespie, meanwhile, is busy shoehorning Rosalie out of Kildare's life, pushing Mary Lamont back into it, and reopening the door of his office to his valued assistant (who has appreciably mellowed from his encounter with life and love).

In **The Secret of Dr. Kildare** the intern is asked to look into a case analogous to that of Barbara Chanler in the first story. Another wealthy young woman, Nancy Messenger, has undergone a sudden drastic personality change, turning from the All-American Girl into a dispirited, compulsive party-goer. Her widowed father is afraid she is going crazy. The case is especially tricky in that she has always had an antipathy to doctors and will resist conventional examinatioin and treatment.

Kildare arranges to be introduced to her incognito and accompanies her on her nightly rounds, hoping she will unconsciously guide him to a solution:

> We will have to wait for some accidental clue—perhaps something she says; perhaps not the words, but the way she speaks them. It may be something as small as a color she likes or shrinks from. Detectives and their crimes--they have an easy time of it--they have a

blood stain—or a body—or a weapon; they have motives printed large enough to serve as headlines. But a case like this—why, she probably doesn't know what drives her to act as she's acting now. If I dared to ask her direct questions, I doubt that she'd be able to give me the answers even if she wanted to.

Clues do turn up. One has already been mentioned: Nancy Messenger is afraid of doctors. She is also afraid to be alone in the dark of night. Sometimes she imagines she's alone in a world of horrible ghosts. She is said to look just like her mother, and her mother is said to have died at the hands of blundering doctors. She has given up horseback riding and other forms of strenuous exercise. She has headaches. Well, by now Kildare should certainly have figured it out, but in fact it takes a chat with a local quack who's wormed his way into her confidence to tip him to the fact that Nancy Messenger expects to die very soon of a brain tumor just like the one that drove her mother mad and then killed her.

The solution to that mystery doesn't set matters right, however, for Ms. Messenger has run off, possibly to wait for death, possibly to hurry it along. Kildare traces her to a childhood hideaway, but there he is faced with a new medical puzzle: she has gone blind. When tests indicate that there is no physical injury to her eyes or her brain, Kildare correctly diagnoses hysterical blindness and stages a charade which snaps her out of it and returns her, happy and healthy, to her father and fiance. Q.E.D.

This case unfortunately gives some prime examples of Kildare's lack of expertise in the detective business. He lets himself get sidetracked when Paul Messenger balks at talking about his wife and her death, thereby missing that essential clue and almost losing his patient altogether. As in other cases, he gets a lot of prompting from Gillespie—in this instance, the old doctor chooses to lecture on hysterical paralysis when he has reason to believe Kildare will be in the auditorium (his assistance being given in this indirect fashion because just at that moment he and Kildare are not on speaking terms). And—dare I say it?—Kildare seems to get a good deal of assistance from his author. Or else he does it by telepathy. How else to explain his certainty that Nancy Messenger will now go and throw herself from the convenient railroad trestle? And how lucky that the remote spot she does pick as a refuge happens to be mentioned again and again to him in conversation! But, under the circumstances, this is quibbling. My thesis is not that Kildare is a great detective, but that he's in there pitching.

On the positive side, he does a bit of successful armchair deduction about the nature of the case before ever meeting his patient, and in more than one instance he excels at playing a part to circumvent his patients' defenses. Kildare seems to be cured of his earlier fault of focussing on symptoms to the exclusion of people: Nancy Messenger and her family are real to him. Still, he never turns into a terribly acute judge of fallen human nature. As his friend Mike the bartender once indulgently explained, "He's just a damn young fool. He don't know anything. He thinks everybody that smiles is a nice guy and the ones that don't smile, they're sick and he'll help them." He's particularly hopeless at figuring women out. Somehow he manages to get along without any worldly wisdom.

"Dr. Kildare's Search" is a manhunt—or, rather, a woman-hunt—far outside the realm of ordinary hospital duties. In this case, the example of Kildare's high-handed attitude toward regulations has inspired a neurosurgeon to perform an emergency operation on an accident victim named Henry Thornton against his will. Upon recovering consciousness, Thornton begins to rave--he says he's been trapped in the wrong day of the week! It's assumed that the surgeon has bungled the operation, and Kildare feels obligated to share the responsibility. He remembers, though, that the patient had been talking oddly even before the operation, and he believes that Thornton's mental troubles are separate from the accident and its treatment. As in earlier cases, Kildare decides to track down the source of the patient's obsession, establish that he was incompetent to refuse permissions for the operation, save the neurosurgeon's reputation (and his own), and perhaps provide a basis for curing the patient's mental problems.

Since Thornton had been brought in without any identification except his name, Kildare's first step is to locate his home--which he does by the time-honored device of tracing the reddish mud from his shoes! Kildare has the grace to feel like a fool doing it, but he takes his mud to the Natural History Museum, where he learns, by the luckiest chance in the world, that it is uniquely to be found in one area of the suburbs. Finding the house, Kildare breaks in, snoops around, and deduces (from the condition of a woman's protrait and other objects) that Thornton is on the verge of being reunited with the wife from whom he has been separated for several years. With a rather dramatic medical treatment he manages to bring Thornton to a brief period of lucidity and gets one clear sentence from him: "I meet Marian--in the lobby of the Clerfayt Hotel--at noon, Friday." In some undisclosed manner (I suspect either auctorial assistance or the help of a superb travel agent), Kildare locates the hotel with that odd name (the more odd since Kildare has never seen it written out) somewhere near Denver, and he brings back the woman for the love of whom Thornton had been losing his mind.

With the woman he loves by his side, Thronton's mental troubles are now on the mend; his neurosurgeon is vindicated; and Kildare can go back to diagnostic medicine.

From here on, Kildare's efforts at detection trail off a bit. The main case in **Dr. Kildare Takes Charge** iinvolves the establishment of a medical clinic in a poor-but-proud Connecticut town and doesn't require any sleuthing, but Kildare does take a page from Holmes's book to solve an urgent case in New York. He has befriended a young couple, Marguerite Paston and William Carew (son of the hospital's head), who are painfully young, idealistic, defenseless, and in love. Being too poor to marry, too besotted to stay apart, and too high-minded to settle for something in between, they make a suicide pact. By a series of unlucky chances, Kildare doesn't learn about their decision until they're long gone. How is he to find them in the metropolis? He comes up with the local equivalent of the Baker Street Irregulars! Kildare is a popular character in Hell's Kitchen, the hospital's neighborhood, and he has no trouble engaging the services of the local kids to search for the missing pair. They find them spending a few last hours together down by the river, and Kildare reaches them just in time. With a little plain talking to them, and especially to Carew's hide-bound father, he gives them a future worth living for. Kildare's days of non-involvement are long gone.

In **Dr. Kildare's Crisis**, wheelchair-bound Gillespie uses ambulance driver Joe Weyman the way Kildare had used the neighborhood kids, to search the streets and locate a pair of fugitives. Apart from this and a few remarks comparing Kildare's genius for diagnosis with a detective's observant eye or a hunting dog's keenness of scent, there's nothing for us in this book. It principally concerns Kildare's attempt to diagnose and save Douglas Lamont, an erratic social philosopher who is the brother of Kildare's fiancee, Mary. Nor is there any detecrtive work to speak of in **Dr. Kildare's Trial,** though Gillespie does give a nice display of medical observation and deduction when he diagnoses the conditions of a boxful of jurors from halfway across the courtroom, while getting Kildare off the hook for an ill-timed bit of Good Samaritanism.

In the last story of the series, "Dr. Kildare's Hardest Case," Kildare uses both a bit of logic and a lot of legwork to track down the cause of a mysterious ailment crippling the Navy Yard. It starts with an accident case—Henry Jervis, a senior Navy engineer, has taken a fall in bad weather at a construction site. On examination, though, Kildare decides that Jervis had been sick before he fell. Then another Navy man has a fall on a calm, clear day. Had something made him dizzy? Are there others? Is there a common denominator? Kildare makes the round of the Navy Yard looking and asking questions. Eventually he finds another case and a link, and from them comes the name of the disease and a cure.

With this piece of medical war work, the Kildare saga comes to an end. Though his true career and the main focus of the stories is medical, Kildare has acquitted himself respectably as an amateur sleuth.

When we consider the history of detective fiction, we can see that the diagnostician-as-detective is a natural. The very profession of fictional private consulting detective is, in part, a legacy to us from Dr. Joseph Bell, consulting surgeon to the Royal Infirmary in Edinburgh in the late 1800s. One of his students wrote of him:

> He was a very skilful surgeon, but his strong point was diagnosis, not only of disease, but of occupation and character. . . . I had ample chance of studying his methods of noticing that he often learned more of the patient by a few quick glances than I had done by my questions.

The author of this encomium was, of course, Arthur Conan Doyle, and he made it plain how much his depiction of the immortal reasoner Sherlock Holmes owed to the skills of Dr. Bell. Holmes' quick eye for detail, his fund of abstruse information, and his logic were gifts to him from the doctor who created him and from that doctor's teacher.

So, it is appropriate to see some of these same gifts passed back to transform another doctor into a part-time sleuth. In "Dr Kildare's Hardest Case," one of Kildare's friends makes explicit the link between the two professions:

> He had seen in Kildare, through the years, every kindness, every patient understanding and human devotion, but under or above the human there was this other soul that lived on the trail like a cat for the kill. The comparison made no sense, Weyman felt, for the purpose of Kildare was always to save and to cure; it was merely that the deepest hunger of all that possessed the doctor was to discover the truth; like an ascetic detective, he consumed himself night and day with a passion to solve the enigmas of disease.

NOTES

[1] The stories' internal chronology is consistent with their original publishing sequence, which was: **Young Dr. Kildare** as a three-part serial in **Argosy** beginning 17 December 1938; **Calling Dr. Kildare** as a three part serial in **Argosy** beginning 25 March 1939; **The Secret of Dr. Kildare** in **Cosmopolitan**, September 1939; "Dr. Kildare's Search" as "Dr. Kildare's Girl" in **Photoplay**, April 1940; **Dr. Kildare Takes Charge** as **Dr. Kildare Goes Home**, a four-part serial in **Argosy** beginning 21 December 1940; **Dr. Kildare's Trial** as **The People vs. Dr. Kildare** in **Cosmopolitan**, May 1941; and "Dr. Kildare's Hardest Case" in **Cosmopolitan**, March 1942. They were published in book form by Dodd, Mead in a slightly different order. "Dr. Kildare's Search" and "Dr. Kildare's Hardest Case" were published together in book form as **Dr. Kildare's Search**. My own reading copies are paperbacks issued by Beagle Books, New York, in 1972.

The Ayres/Barrymore MGM movie versions of these stories were: **Young Dr. Kildare** (1938), **Calling Dr. Kildare** (1939), **The Secret of Dr. Kildare** (1939), **Dr. Kildare's Strange Case** [equivalent to "Dr. Kildare's Search"] (1940), **Dr. Kildare Goes Home** (1940), **Dr. Kildare's Crisis** (1940), and **The People vs. Dr. Kildare** (1941).

The brief story "Dr. Kildare's Hardest Case," published after Faust and MGM had parted company, was never turned into a film. Conversely, Faust naturally did not produce texts for the Ayres/Barrymore vehicles on which he had not collaborated—**Dr. Kildare's Wedding Day** (1941) and **Dr. Kildare's Victory** (1942)—much less the string of films starring Barrymore and various supporters after Lew Ayres departed the screen, and Kildare with him. Sadly, these final films, which continued to appear through 1947, outlived their creator: Frederick Faust was killed in Italy in 1944 while serving as a war correspondent.

My bibliographical and biographical information on Faust comes for the most part from **Max Brand: The Man and His Work**, edited by Darrell C. Richardson (Los Angeles: Fantasy Publishing Co., 1952), particularly the sections by Richardson and by William F. Nolan. Information on the films comes from **The Great Movie Series**, edited by James Robert Parish (South Brunswick, New Jersey: A.S. Barnes, 1971.)

[2] Max Brand's original creation of Dr. Jimmy Kildare was in two short stories, "Interns Can't Take Money" (published in **Cosmopolitan**, March 1936) and "Whiskey Sour" (published in **Cosmopolitan**, April 1938). This young Dr. Kildare aspired to be a surgeon, not a diagnostician; there was no Leonard Gillespie in his world; and it was only his familiar honesty and compassion (without a whit of analytical thinking) that pulled him through two encounters with the likeable crooks of the hospital's neighborhood. The movie **Interns Can't Take Money**, starring Joel McCrea, was released in 1937 by Paramount. When Faust signed on with MGM in 1938, he revamped his characters and restarted the series from Kildare's arrival at the hospital.

Decades later, when an MGM television series chronicled the doings of a contemporary Kildare and Gillespie (played by Richard Chamberlain and Raymond Massey), novels about these characters duly appeared, including **Dr. Kildare** (Lancer, 1962), by Robert Ackworth; **Dr. Kildare's Secret Romance** (Lancer, 1962), and **Dr. Kildare's Finest Hour** (Lancer, 1963), by Norman Daniels; and **Dr. Kildare: The Heart Has an Answer** (Lancer, 1963) and **Dr. Kildare: The Faces of Love** (Lancer, 1963), by William Johnston. Some of these contain a bit of detective work, principally in backtracking patients' histories, but they haven't got the blood and thunder of the Brand books.

[3]Sir Arthur Conan Doyle, **Memories and Adventures** (London: Hodder & Stoughton, 1924), p. 25.

[Continued from page 1]
that I was doing him a favor by letting him do those things for me.

Only one time was I ever able to do anything for him in return, and my eyes moisten at the memory of how he reacted. Shortly after **TMF** 3:4 came out, Jud wrote to say how much he liked the portrait of Nero Wolfe which adorned that issue's cover. The drawing, which had been done for me by an elderly man who was also a fan of Rex Stout and his most famous creation, was quite large—possibly eighteen by twenty-four inches—and sat above the mantel in my living room. I took it down the day I received Jud's note and shipped it to him the next day, and the joy I felt in possessing the portrait was nothing compared to the joy that came from giving it to Jud. When it arrived Jud was ecstatic, and he immediately gave it a place of honor in the room of his home which was devoted to his Stout collection and to which he referred as "The Shrine."

I still have three books that Jud loaned me by mail a few months before he knew of his illness. They sit atop a shelf in my cluttered office, wrapped in the great wads of protective plastic in which Jud sent them to me. I'll have to send them back to Linda soon, but I think I'll hold onto them for a while longer.

Another death to report is that of Desmond Bagley, who died in mid-April just short of his sixtieth birthday. Jane Bakerman interviewed Bagley when she was recently in Europe, and her account of that interview in this issue of **TMF** is a memorial to this gifted and prolific writer.

You do not need to be told that this issue of **TMF** is late, and the reason for its lateness lies before your eyes. After several years of looking at and yearning for a computer on which to produce this magazine, I finally made the plunge. That was a couple of months ago, and I've spent much of the time since then trying to master the beast. My geographical isolation here in southern Indiana, hours away from the nearest specialist in this particular brand of electronic wizardry, has meant that I have had to be both teacher and student, and my progress has been painfully slow. But I think that I've got the hang of it now (more or less), and in the long run the machine should save me great amounts of time at the same time that it produces what I hope you will agree is great-looking copy.

To get back on schedule, I plan to turn right around and put 7:3 together as soon as 7:2 is taken care of, so your next issue should follow this one in a matter of weeks, not months. After that I have every hope of being able to get back on and stick to a regular schedule. Who knows, I might even revive the long-neglected policy of publishing deadlines for future issues.

The World of Nero Wolfe

Asbjørn Skytte

[Translated by E.F. Bleiler
from the article in the
Danish magazine, **Pinkerton.**]

    Nero Wolfe is one of the most remarkable private detectives in the literature of crime. He lives in a large, distinguished, and well-run sandstone house on West 35th Street in New York. He does not like to leave his house--on principle, he is unwilling to do so for business purposes--just as he hates any sort of change and has a very wide distrust of all the mechanical phenomena of the modern world, like trains, airplanes, and autos. He is intellectually brilliant, and his sharp wit and faculty for precise formulation are combined with an arrogant insolence which borders on total contempt for the remainder of mankind--especially for women in general.
    Wolfe has four great interests, which he cultivates uninhibitedly. He is incredibly well read and is expert in the history of literature; he tends orchids on the roof of his house (from nine to eleven in the morning and from four to six in the afternoon); he is a great gourmet and he has one of the best cooks in the world employed in his kitchen, where together they work out the elaborate menus; and finally, he drinks beer with systematic singleness of purpose. These last two interests contribute to the fact that he weighs more than 140 kg. Naturally, this only increases his laziness and stubborn reluctance to move about any more than is absolutely necessary.
    In his genius and extreme eccentricity Nero Wolfe can be compared to his English colleagues Sherlock Holmes and Lord Peter Wimsey. (W.S. Baring-Gould, however, in his biography **Nero Wolfe of West Thirty-Fifth Street**, proposes the theory that Wolfe is Holmes's illegitimate son.) Like Holmes, Wolfe has a trusted collaborator who is at the same time his chronicler and the first-person narrator of his books. But here the likeness ends. Archie Goodwin is not just a faithful, admiring, and astonished narrator who records, with meticulous politeness, the merits of genius. Goodwin is an American and in his hard-boiled narrative style and quick-witted humor is more closely related to the tradition of Chandler and Hammett. And it is in this neat equipoise between the types of the detective story that the Nero Wolfe novels find their distinctive quality and their vitality.
    Archie Goodwin is in many ways Wolfe's direct opposite: considerably younger, full of witty wisecracks and impulsive ideas, appreciative of women, sober, and well groomed. He is an excellent secretary who can take shorthand letters as fast as Wolfe can dictate them, and an equally fine errand boy who attends to the leg work on the outside and can then return with an exact repetition of hour-long conversations among up to half a score of people who are involved. But above all else Goodwin serves as a mediator to the reader for a boss who with his conservatism and misanthropic hatred of women is

really completely intolerable, and who thus is completely dependent on Archie in all areas.

Beyond these two chief personages, the novels operate with an unusually large, established group of characters. In the house also lives the cook, Fritz Brenner, together with Theodore Horstmann, who helps take care of the orchids. Outside, Wolfe often draws upon the work of three freelance detectives: Saul Panzer, who is always presented as a perfect fellow worker and who is also Archie's poker companion; Fred Durkin, and Orrie Cather, who are more fallible, the last named, however, being unsympathetically characterized. Sometimes there is a fourth man along with them: Bill Gore in the early novels and Johnny Keems in the later. Similarly established are the chief personages in Homicide: Sergeant Stebbins, Lieutenant Rowcliff, and most of all Inspector Cramer, who as a rule is in direct conflict with Wolfe and time after time threatens to revoke Archie's license or put him in jail. Cramer is choleric, cigar-chewing, but intelligent enough that on every occasion he bows to Wolfe's manipulations of genius. In addition there is Wolfe's close friend (and perhaps twin brother) Marko Vukcic, who owns Rustermann's Restaurant and is murdered in one of the novels. There is also the newspaper man, Lon Cohen from the **Gazette**, who often hands over information in exchange for scoops from Wolfe. There is Lily Rowan, who is Archie's firm friend and who loves him beyond measure, and finally there are Dr. Vollmer and Parker the lawyer, who deliver, respectively, medical and legal assistance when such is required.

Basically, the novels about Nero Wolfe are stereotyped. In every story there take place one or more murders, which involve a larger number of suspects. Wolfe may be involved from the start--for the first murder--or he may first come into the picture later, often through his own manipulations. Along the way the large cast of characters may be drawn on, according to pleasure or need, until the end, when Wolfe assembles all the concerned persons in his office and unmasks the murderer. It is like a commedia dell'arte play: the nature and function of all the individual players are known in advance, but the possibilities for variation are endless. The inner motivation depends upon the tension set up between the known narrative style (the familiar universe and predictable happenings) and new, surprising combinations within the bounds of the established conventions.

The man behind Nero Wolfe, Rex Stout, was born in 1886. He made his debut late as a writer--in 1927--after having made his fortune in banking and finance. The first Nero Wolfe novel, **Fer-de-Lance**, appeared in 1934, and with, in all, 46 titles, the series amounts to the larger part of the author's work. Thirteen of the volumes were composed of from two to four short pieces, but the remainder are novels. The last, **A Family Affair**, was published in 1975, a month before Rex Stout's death.

The books thus extend chronologically over forty-one years, and if old age does not noticeably catch up with Wolfe and Goodwin, in various ways Stout succeeded in keeping up with the times. The many technical refinements in Wolfe's house come in along the way: the pane of one-way-vision glass in the front door; the secret panel between the hall and the office, from which especially trusted persons can watch Wolfe in action; the hidden tape recorder in Wolfe's desk, etc. Even social developments were mirrored in the novels, the high point being **The Doorbell Rang** (1965), when Wolfe comes into direct conflict with the FBI and where J. Edgar Hoover himself, at the end of the book, stands raging and ringing at the door--but is not admitted.

In several novels a surprise effect is attained by the rare

[Continued on page 26]

An Interview with Desmond Bagley

Jane S. Bakerman

Fans of Desmond Bagley's taut, vivid adventure novels are accustomed to--and mightily pleased with--the care and accuracy with which the exotic settings and the details of daily life in far places are rendered. They are accustomed to Bagley the careful, Bagley the painstaking, Bagley the exact. But in one assessment, Desmond Bagley is dead wrong; wrong when he says that he is "not an extraordinary man." The remark, though, is typical of Bagley's habit of self-deprecation, for, while he is justly proud of the veracity and quality of his novels, he seems not to find it at all unusual that an "ordinary" man has written them. To those of us who read the books, they seem admirable feats indeed; it also seems that the man who wrote them is something very special, and, in this instance, our judgment is far more accurate than his.

To create such novels as **The Golden Keel** (1963), **High Citadel** (1965), **Wyatt's Hurricane** (1966), **Landslide** (1967), **The Vivero Letter** (1968), **The Spoilers** (1969), **Running Blind** (1970), **The Freedom Trap** (1971, also published as **The Macintosh Man**), **The Tightrope Men** (1973), **The Snow Tiger** (1974), **The Enemy** (1977), **Flyaway** (1978), **Bahama Crisis** (1980), and **Windfall** (1982), is a major accomplishment. Avoiding repetition, keeping the subjects and materials fresh, and especially creating fully developed, convincing characters who differ sharply from one another but share the ability to face crises and dangers with guts and honor are clearly the individual factors which make the books so strong and mark Bagley as a leader in the fields of crime-adventure-espionage fiction.

The novels often center upon what one character calls "little gray men," ordinary-seeming people who suddenly find themselves in wildly unusual situations, forced to cope or to die, and it was in speaking of his heroes that Bagley erred in assessing himself. He said:

> I am by no means an extraordinary man, [yet] I find that I've done some extraordinary things: I've been to the South Pole; I've crossed the Sahara three times; I've been to Greenland and other out-of-the-way places. Now, what usually happens is that I talk myself into these things, and all the time it's happening, I'm usually scared as hell! Which is the position in which my heroes often find themselves. The definition of adventure is "fright and discomfort recollected in tranquillity," you see, so ....

Readers do see, and they are the beneficiaries of the writer's willingness to talk himself into "these things"!

The site Bagley and his wife, Joan, have chosen for his recollection in tranquillity is Catel House in St. Andrew, Guernsey, the Channel Islands. The Channel Islands, it seems, meet all the Bagleys' needs for a good place to live. Tax rates are sane, the economy seems sound, and the locale is beautiful. One is never far from the sea, of course; St. Andrews is a thriving town with fairly steeply inclined streets and pleasant-seeming, friendly people. There are, as one would expect, herds of Guernsey cattle grazing in the small fields lying outside the town (no other cattle are allowed to set hoof upon the island, and, interestingly, occasionally new bulls are imported from the U.S. to keep the breed strong), numbers of greenhouses (apparently devoted primarily to tomato growing) dot the landscape, and hordes of tourists appear in summer (despite the erratic plane schedules). Another aspect of the area is far more surprising, however--the island is liberally endowed with military emplacements, most now defunct, dating from Roman times to the World War II era; this feature is a sobering element in an otherwise placid scene and reminds visitors that the dangerous world of war, criminals, pirates, spies, and natural disaster (all reflected in Bagley's fiction) is not, after all, very far away.

In the many front windows of the Bagley home, their several pets often sit to keep an eye on the action--or mourn the departure of their owners--and the house lies fairly close to the narrow (by American standards) street. It's a pretty neighborhood--quiet, ultra-well-kept homes, very attractive. The entire house, in fact, gives a sense of peacefulness and purpose. The walls are light, and, though there are lots of souveniers and gadgets (all very useful: word processor, video tape recorder, all manner of intriguing devices in the kitchen) about, the home feels spacious and uncluttered, comfortable and welcoming. The back yard is large and is a masterpiece of gardening skill.

At the time I was there, Bagley's study, which was in the process of renovation, was actually a kind of suite up on the second floor. His word processor, which he regards as a real boon in his work and which he will patiently demonstrate at the drop of a hint, dominated a good-sized, bright room whose windows overlook the back garden and its greenhouse. Across the word-processor room, and a step up, there's another long, pleasant room, one wall almost completely glass, most of the others lined with bookcases. On a clear day he can see the coast of France from this second room, the original study.

The personal reference library the Bagleys have amassed is excellent ("Practically everything in here has got something to do with my work") and ranges from almanacks through dictionaries (Spanish, French, Welsh, Japanese, Maori, for instance), atlases, math books, to technical manuals: **Signs of Crime, A Field Manual for Police; A Guide to Private Detection; The Flyer's Handbook;** and **How to Abandon Ship** (bought for twenty cents in Los Angeles).

> I compliment myself that I have built up a library where I can find everything in my own home, without going to a public library.... I have never had my hero to abandon a ship at sea, but if I ever have that, I can go to this shelf here and get that book.... There's nobody so quick on the draw with a ballpoint pen as a reader who finds out a writer in an error of fact--which is why I have to take immense precautions and do research.

Experts as well as fans recognize Bagley's precise use of facts; the accuracy of **Wyatt's Hurricane**, for example, has been warmly endorsed in a review in the **Bulletin of the American Meteorological Society** and in "**Wyatt's Hurricane:** A Meteorological Critique."

The study also boasts a sign: "It's Hard to Be Humble When You're as Great as I Am," established there, visitors are told, by Joan Bagley, who usually accompanies her husband on his travels. She is, he reports, the better sailor of the pair, and she strikes one as an open, friendly woman wearing an air of very great competence very unassumingly.

Also on display in the study are artifacts any fan would recognize immediately: a Raamen rope doll (one figures in **The Tightrope Men**—it's a friendlier-looking doll than I had thought from reading the book), a mirror/tray (prototype of the key clue in **The Vivero Letter**), and a circular throwing knife (as used in **Flyaway**; it's rusty, just as described in the novel, and the "skimming" throw Bagley pantomimes to demonstrate it is a little like the pitch of a good Frisbee player); these are a few examples. Bagley collects most of them on site, of course. He comments that in one sense place sometimes comes first in his novels: "I go to the place, and if it has any prospects, I write," and, generally, this method is eminently workable. At least once, though, it aborted: "I have been to the South Pole, and I have tried to write a novel on the Antarctic eight times. Last year I wrote a complete novel and scrapped it! It's very painful."

When the system **does** work, however, the results are terrific, and Bagley recognizes its importance in his work.

> When I started to write, I could not afford to go to the places which I was writing about. The first novel that I researched on the ground was **Running Blind**, set in Iceland. I went to Iceland. I traveled all over Iceland, and I hope I have drawn a picture of the most peculiar society which I encountered there. You see, in my books, the environment acts as another character. And **Running Blind** could have happened nowhere else except in Iceland.

The amalgamation between plot and setting is indeed so complete in **Running Blind** that the arid landscape and the habits of life seem useful symbols of the tension felt by the hero, betrayed and rebetrayed, but Bagley sees it otherwise:

> **Running Blind** was a joke! I was trying to satirize espionage.... I mean, I had a spy master running both sides of the operation, and how much more satiric can you get than that? But, you see, it is impossible to satirize the CIA or the British Intelligence or the KGB because what they are doing in practice is as unbelievable as fiction! I mean, if you have as happened to a man in London: he was poked in his leg with an umbrella which injected a poison pellet, and he died ... **That happened**!

Even when fact isn't outdoing fancy, the assimilation process can take considerable time. For instance, Bagley mentioned that while working on one of several current projects, an autobiography (working title, **Writer**), he had

> been going through a lot of old correspondence and files, and I came across a letter to my editor in which I told

him I was going to write a novel about an avalanche. Now, that letter was dated 1963; the novel about the avalanche [**The Snow Tiger**] was published in 1974, and you might ask what was happening in the meantime. Well, the short answer is that I didn't know anything about avalanches, and I had to find out--and it took me ten years!

According to its author, **The Snow Tiger** also includes "a lot of the information I got in the Antarctic.... I've cannibalized... I've taken extracts from the books which I've abandoned and incorporated them into other books--all the great musicians have done it, so why can't authors?"

This sort of borrowing is one way of dealing with writer's block. When that problem occurs, Bagley doesn't yield to it.

I just keep trying.... Writer's block is a very tragic thing. It isn't usually fatal, but it can be a very miserable thing. And I've had it. As you write, trying to make each novel a bit better than the last, it becomes harder, and you can't always pull it off. And I've had the floor of my study strewn with the corpses of unfinished books.

Generally, Bagley keeps to a regular schedule, trying for a set number of pages per day--

Well, I try; sometimes it comes off; sometimes it doesn't. Sometimes it flows; other times, it's hard work. I work office hours: half past 9 to half past 5, five days a week; I take the weekends off....

I actually drive Joan out of her tiny mind because I end my work at the end of a page, even if I am in the middle of a sentence. She reads my day's production as a sort of cliff-hanger, and she comes to the end of a page in the middle of a sentence, and it drives her nuts!

Characterization, like a steady schedule, is also central to Bagley's interest and method: "For each character, I have his own history here [in his head]--not just what he does in the book, but the family he was born into, and his life before he entered the picture. It helps to round it off." His plans for a new novel are also "all in the head."

I sometimes make an outline, but it's an inward outline. If you have a synopsis, you're putting yourself into a sort of straight jacket, and you might have to make a character perform an action which you **know** that that character would not perform.

Look, I start a novel with an interesting situation; that is chapter one. And I intend that the novel should end over there.... The characters react against each other and with the particular environment which they are in. And it's a result of this that the plot of the book grows organically--like a tree.

Now I originally intended the novel to end **there**, but it might end over **there**, at complete right angles to my original intention, but that's **okay**, as long as it's got there naturally.

At least once, though, a complex plot was the entire genesis of a novel, proving that for its author, as for most good writers, creativity is a matter of discipline and good, solid work, rather than a matter of some mysterious force called "inspiration."

> I once started to write a novel called **The Tightrope Men**, and I started to write it because the time had come to write a novel, because my publisher expected a novel. I sat down at the typewriter with three hundred sheets of blank paper and an equally blank mind. I didn't have a clue; I didn't have an idea. So I wrote seven pages, describing the most improbable situation in which a man could possibly find himself: he wakes up in a strange room, in a strange country, goes into the bathroom, looks into the mirror and sees a strange face-- And it took the rest of the novel to get myself out of the corner which I'd painted myself into! So the short answer is that you do not need inspiration!

Unlike many other crime-espionage-adventure writers, Desmond Bagley doesn't do short stories:

> Oh, I've tried. In fact, I've written in my autobiography something about how a person starts to write. He starts off with poetry because it's short. He thinks it's easy, and he finds out that it isn't as easy as he thought it was. Then he goes on to short stories, which again are short. And he thinks they're easy, but they aren't. And then, a novel is the easiest of all, actually--all you need is stamina and time!

Stamina and time are certainly essential ingredients, but Bagley also concentrates pretty intensely on structure. **Running Blind**, for instance, was rebuilt. As it now stands, the opening premise is the extreme difficulty of getting rid of a dead body.

> [But] the original novel didn't start that way. Then, I had a look at the book, and I said, if I can start in the middle of the action, it would be terrific. So I re-jigged the book to start in the middle of the action, and then did a flashback in order to state why.
>
> The flashback technique is not to be recommended for the beginner. It's awfully hard to handle; for example, **The Snow Tiger** was all in flashbacks, all the way through. At one point in the first draft, I discovered that I had a flashback inside a flashback! **Then** I decided, No! I can't have that!

Every author has, in one sense, a collaborator, his editor, and Bagley's editor sees each manuscript fairly early on:

> I've had the same editor for eighteen years, and we have come to a modus operandi which is strange, but it works. I write the first draft; now, it has a lot of imperfections: it's got a lot of spelling errors, a lot of grammatical errors--I might have changed my mind about

something in the middle, so that the first half of the novel doesn't hinge into the second half. But in spite of all that, I give my editor the first draft, and he reads it. He's got to know me as a writer--that I'm quite aware of all these imperfections--and then I say, "If you have any comments to make, any suggestions for improvement, have them now, before I write the second draft, because the second draft is going to be the final draft."
   The editorial session, after he's read the first draft, usually lasts an hour. That's all. And I leave him. In the normal course of events, most of the suggestions that he makes I've already thought of. The suggestions that he makes which I think will improve the novel are incorporated; any other suggestions I ignore, because I am the person whose name is on the jacket, not my editor....

While the name is going on the jacket, however, the author is suffering a kind of painful withdrawal--

   Well, I'll tell you exactly how it is: if you take a rubber band and stretch it between your thumbs, and it gets tighter and tighter, and then somebody comes along with a pair of scissors and snips it off-- After I've finished a novel, I wander around the house feeling rather like a spare part--depressed ....

Developing the novels has clearly become a carefully organized, practical process as well as a creative one. Now a successful practitioner of the work he loves, Bagley can joke about it. When asked if his characters reflect himself, he replied, "No, I pattern myself after my characters. I always feel as old as my latest hero--running now, about the age of forty-two...." But it wasn't always obvious that writing would--or should--be his career:

   Because I came from a north of England working class family, the idea of writing to earn a living was knocked on the head hard. My parents could not possibly see how anybody could earn a living by putting words on paper.
   I didn't have a formal education--I have never passed an academic examination! The world is full of people who would have liked to have written a novel,... but they're not prepared to go through the whole sweaty process. If you can write, you will write! And I left school at the age of fourteen and a half; as a matter of fact, I ran away from school ....
   I was an apprentice to a printer, and during the war I worked in the aircraft industry, making bits and pieces of airplanes.
   Then, after the war, I emigrated to South Africa--drove all the way--[even] across the Sahara. There was a whole crowd of us. You see, after the war, a lot of people wanted to leave England. The shipping line from London to Cape Town was booked up for two years, and the airlines was booked up for a year and a half, so it was the only thing to do!

To Bagley, perhaps, this decision to drive across two continents
                                                    [Continued on page 26]

Deduction in Duplicate

Alan S. Mosier

One of the curious trends of the so-called "Sherlock Holmes Boom" of the mid to late 1970's was the composition and publication of pastiches in pairs.

A pastiche, for those unfamiliar with the term, is a serious effort at imitating the style of one particular author, using his characters and settings to create a reasonable facsimile.

My collection (by no means complete) of Holmes pastiches numbers thirty volumes published during the "boom" years. The quality varies from downright disgusting (Aubrey's **Sherlock Holmes in Dallas**) to efforts that Conan Doyle would have been proud to have penned himself (Boyer's **Giant Rat of Sumatra**).

The question that puzzles me about the pairs of pastiches that sit on my shelf is not why the authors chose to write more than one--that can be easily answered in most cases: money--but how any self-respecting publishers came to let some of these out under their imprints!

These pairs are worth a look, if only for the fact that their authors occupied the mainstream of Sherlockian fiction for the best part of eight years.

In examining these pairs, one must start with the work of a man who, almost single-handedly, initiated the boom with his trend-setting Seven-per-cent Solution in 1974. Nicholas Meyer, who has also directed several films (**Time After Time, Star Trek II: The Wrath of Kahn**), instituted a pattern that was followed with unfortunate lack of imagination on the part of subsequent writers. He paired Sherlock Holmes with a historical personality, Sigmund Freud. This well-thought-out and interesting book was later turned into a movie, and its success prompted a sequel entitled **The West End Horror** (1976). Unfortunately, it also prompted a spate of imitations that paired the master sleuth with the likes of Bertrand Russell, Harry Houdini, and Theodore Roosevelt!

Meyer himself feels that **The West End Horror**, although not containing as good an idea as Holmes meets Freud, is in itself a more satisfying mystery. I must agree. While it too has the "Holmes meets ..." syndrome on display, it is not so dependent on the idea and is truer to the style and feel of the original sixty tales of Doyle.

Meyer's style recalls that of Doyle (he even uses some of Doyle's key words and phrases to remind the reader that this is a Holmes tale), and he never oversteps the bounds of credibility or good taste. Neither effort descends to the level of parody.

But the next pair of pastiches gleefully does. Austin Mitchelson and Nicholas Utechin released two works in 1976. Both stretch one's credulity beyond the breaking point. In **The Earthquake Machine** we travel with Holmes to Russia for a demonstration staged for Tsar Nicholas (the Meyer Syndrome again!) of the first nuclear device, devised by the evil genius Tremaris (a.k.a. Professor Moriarty), who eventually is done away with--this time by the faithful Watson.

If Holmes-Meets-the-A-Bomb isn't bad enough, their second effort is even more outrageous. **Hellbirds** takes place in 1914, using **His Last Bow** as its point of departure. Having already eliminated the infamous Professor in their last book, Mitchelson and Utechin turn to the dastardly German spy Von Bork this time out. This incredible adventure sees Holmes and Watson pursue the German agent behind the front lines of World War I and return through the air after dueling with Baron Manfred Von Richtofen with Holmes as pilot! So much for Holmes's quiet retirement on the Sussex Downs. We can only wonder how these two books came to be released. The authors would seem to subscribe to the theory that the wilder the plot device, the better.

Our next pair of pastiches uses what we must call literary license, for they chronicle the encounters between Holmes and other fictitious characters.

The year 1978 brought with it **Sherlock Holmes Vs. Dracula: Or, The Adventure of the Sanguinary Count**, by Loren D. Estleman. It is more or less a retelling of the English episodes of Bram Stoker's **Dracula**, with Holmes involved in tracking down the fiend and sending him off to Transylvania. Once one has accepted Estleman's premise, the book is fairly amusing and offers a relaxed imitation of Doyle's style. If one has read **Dracula**, the story is less than surprising. It at least has a certain charm and can be read quickly.

Estleman (or his agent) liked the literary license idea enough to follow up the first volume with a second entitled **Dr. Jekyll and Mr. Holmes** (1979). This one has Holmes and Watson embroiled with Henry Jekyll's split personality. Holmes gets off a few good ones at the expense of Robert Louis Stevenson and deduces his way through the requisite number of pages to the climactic scene in Jekyll's lab. The most amusing part of this pastiche is Estleman's explanation of how he came into possession of the manuscript.

Frank Thomas plays bridge and reads Sherlock Holmes. He combined the two in **Sherlock Holmes, Bridge Detective, Returns**. Then he dropped the bridge. In 1979 Pinnacle paperbacks brought out his **Sherlock Holmes and the Golden Bird**. This clone of **The Maltese Falcon** makes Holmes a world traveler and falls somewhere between Meyer and Mitchelson in credibility. He adds a dash of Estleman (Chu San Fu; a thinly veiled version of Fu Manchu) to complete the picture.

Thomas--among others--seems to feel it necessary to remove Holmes from "that sceptered Isle," and so we find him in pursuit of the Golden Bird, following a trail that leads to Berlin and Constantinople. Thomas (re)introduces several characters from earlier bridge outings: a gentleman named Orloff, and a reformed thief. Orloff makes another appearance in **Sherlock Holmes and the Sacred Sword** (1980), the second in Thomas's pair. Having already secured the Golden Bird, Holmes is now trying to prevent a holy war by recovering the sword of the prophet, stolen from the residence of the infamous Captain Spaulding, African explorer.

In both books, Thomas gives more than the customary share of the glory to Watson, no stooge he! The doctor plays just as important a part as Holmes. This goes a long way in regard to saving the book. I mean, really! Holmes discovering the tomb of King Tut years before Howard Carter?

The preceding pairs have all dealt with Holmes as the

protagonist. The following feature him only as an extra and are not pastiches in the strictest sense of the word. The limelight is occupied by Professor James Moriarty. One pair regards him as Doyle intended he should be--The Napoleon of Crime --the other as a more human, but mis-directed, man.

John Gardner's **Return of Moriarty** (1974) merits special attention. Its atmosphere of pervading evil is realistic and presented in an entertaining and sometimes frightening form. Moriarty is the Godfather of London, a cold, calculating computer of criminality. Holmes plays only a small part in the tale, but Gardner's view of the inner workings of Moriarty's world is so fascinating that we hardly miss him. Along with Meyer, John Gardner has hit the nail on the head in the matter of style and content. This book is so far superior to the drivel that characterized the boom years that no self-respecting Sherlockian need be ashamed to put it on his shelf next to the Canon itself.

Only slightly less satisfying, **The Revenge of Moriarty** (1975) takes up where the previous book leaves off. Sherlock Holmes is more in evidence here; in fact, his addiction to cocaine is one of the important plot devices. Gardner's use of this device differs completely from Meyer's view of the same subject. How Holmes shakes off his addiction rings true to Doyle.

There was to be a third book entitled **The Revolt of Moriarty**, but, sadly, John Gardner was killed in an accident before the project could be brought to fruition.

Perhaps it will be Michael Kurland that makes it a trilogy with his own Moriarty series. Appearing in 1979, **The Infernal Device** paints a diametrically opposed portrait of the Professor. He is actually involved in helping Holmes thwart a plot against her Majesty's life. His rescue of a news reporter in a clever and droll manner set the tone for this lighter-hearted look at Victorian crime. Kurland writes with an easy style that lends itself well to the tale he tells. He has created a Watson for Moriarty: Benjamin Barnett, the rescued reporter who in turn for his release from prison must serve Moriarty for two years, no questions asked. This does not particularly bother Barnett, as he sees the Professor as the sort of man who answers to a higher authority than British law. In Kurland's view, Holmes had an **idee fixe** concerning the doings of the Professor. He saw Moriarty's nefarious hand in every crime committed. Interesting, but not highly flattering.

Death by Gaslight (1982) finds Moriarty, Barnett, Holmes, and company pursuing a murderer that specializes in cutting the throats of England's more sexually depraved aristocracy. A sub-plot involves the robbery and recovery of a vast Indian treasure. This book is superior to the first, in that Kurland is more at home in his characterizations.

Again, Kurland's work is not strictly pastiche, as there is no aping of the style of Conan Doyle. He even goes so far as to write a disclaimer at the beginning. However, it is something of a sham, for the learned Sherlockian will find some of Holmes's best-known phrases issuing from the lips of his nemesis!

As in the case of Gardner, a third novel, entitled **The Murder Trust**, is in the works and is slated to appear sometime this year.

Of the ten books mentioned in the proceeding pages, I would rate Meyer's **Seven-per-cent Solution** and Gardner's **Return of Moriarty** at the top of my list. There is always room for interesting and knowledgeable speculation. At the other end of the spectrum repose the two volumes by Messrs. Mitchelson and Utechin, works with no redeeming values whose main purpose was to cash in on the boom. Hopefully they fell short of achieving their economic goals.

[Continued on page 30]

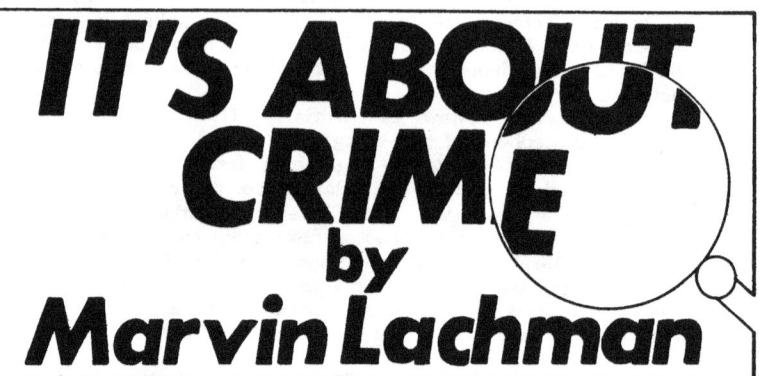

IT'S ABOUT CRIME by Marvin Lachman

NOTES ON RECENT READING

My favorite growth industry is the publication of books **about** the mystery. From the rare title before 1967, we have expanded to the plethora that so pleasantly plagued readers in 1982.

Two of these books are merely indexes. I say "merely," but as John Nieminski, David Doerrer, and Steve Stilwell know full well it is no easy job compiling an index that is both complete and correct. As yet, I have found no errors of either omission or commission in Ruth Tanis Hall's **Dorothy Sayers: A Reference Guide** (G.K. Hall & Co., 70 Lincoln St., Boston, MA 02111, $27.50) or E.R. Hagemann's **Comprehensive Index to Black Mask, 1920-1951** (Bowling Green University Popular Press, Bowling Green, OH 43403, hardcover $15.95, paperback $8.95). The latter book is especially useful to devotees of the pulps and short stories since, in addition to listing every story that appeared in that legendary magazine, it also charts the various series characters and tells a bit--e.g., their locale--about many of them.

I'm a bit sorry that some of the wrong academic types have discovered the mystery, since they have produced works that are usually boring and display little of the love for the mystery that many of us have. A case in point is **The Pursuit of Crime: Art and Ideology in Detective Fiction** by Dennis Porter, published by Yale University Press (no price on dust jacket), which combines academic jargon with some basic errors. Why does Mr. Porter say that Dupin's first name was Claude? Have I been missing something all these years, or is he thinking of the old French actor, Claude Dauphin?

Robin Winks is an academic, all right. He teaches history at Yale and reviews mysteries for **The New Republic**. But he clearly loves mysteries. His latest book is **Modus Operandi**, from David R. Godine (306 Dartmouth St., Boston, MA 02116, $$12.50). At times Winks seems almost afraid of his love and searches throughout for more acceptable--i.e., academic--reasons for reading them.

Thus, Winks joins others who say one reason for reading mysteries is their "cathartic effect." I believe that those who say that need a laxative. He does not seem to accept mystery fiction as escape fiction, and thus criticizes John Dickson Carr for his lack of reality, missing Carr's escape-valve values as a writer. Winks writes very well, as in his excellent chapter on spy fiction. At times, though, he embarrasses us (and himself) with sentences that are so long as to be confusing. See two of these on page 101. He also says that writers for the fanzines are not serious critics of detective fiction.

Outrageous and wrong-headed though he may be, Winks's **Modus Operandi** is never dull and can be recommended for those willing to let a little controversy into their lives. And, after all, any essayist who criticizes Edmund Wilson can't be all bad.

Which Way Did He Go?, by Edward Margolies (Holmes & Meier, Inc., 30 Irving Place, New York, NY 10003, no price on book), is a paperback more designed to appeal to academics or even to be used as the text in a course on the hard-boiled mystery. Margolies covers four writers, three of whom have been done to death by the "publish or perish" school: Hammett, Chandler, and Ross Macdonald. Because Chester Himes is popular with intellectuals, Margolies has added him, though the subtitle of the book refers to it being about The Private Eye. The last time I looked, Coffin Ed Johnson and Grave Digger Jones were **police** detectives, albeit unconventional ones. There is very little here that is new for readers of this publication, but those less familiar with the genre will get a great deal out of this book, so feel free to recommend it to "beginners."

Few books do a better job of conveying the fun in reading mysteries than Bill Pronzini's **Gun in Cheek** (Putnam, $15.95). He especially finds bad mysteries to be fun and establishes a sub-genre, "alternate classics," those books which are much worse than the "good bad books" Boucher used to write about, but they are redeemed by their unintentionally funny lines. Incidentally, as Jimmy Durante used to say, "Everyone wants to get into the act." Ed McBain has done an unnecessary three-page introduction to **Gun in Cheek** in which he claims to have been a writer of bad lines. From the examples he gives, McBain was never bad, or funny, enough.

But the authors who Pronzini chose to exemplify his "classics" are bad and funny enough, e.g., Michael Avallone, Sydney Horler, and Sean O'Shea (who once wrote that deathless line, "She bugged my belly button."). A few of Pronzini's examples go on too long, and he gives away many endings. Normally, I object to that, but these are books I probably would not read anyway, so his synopses have saved me time and given me a lot of laughs.

Bill, did you really read fifty-seven Fleming Stone books?

Ely M. Liebow, Associate Professor of English at Northeastern Illinois University, has all the academic credentials to be boring; he is not. He has found a marvelous subject for a biography in **Dr. Joe Bell: Model for Sherlock Holmes** (Bowling Green University Popular Press, cloth $25.95, paper $10.95). Liebow's research seems impeccable, and his writing is lively, especially his chapter titles. Who else could work a classic line about the Chicago White Sox scandal into a biography of a Scottish M.D.?

In addition to telling us much about the man who indirectly has been responsible for as much pleasure as almost anyone who ever lived, Liebow presents us with some fascinating details regarding the teaching and practice of medicine in nineteenth-century Edinburgh. Liebow's last chapter, though he tries to be generous, points up the smallness of **Adrian** Conan Doyle, the unworthy son of a genuinely great man.

George Dove has written about as comprehensive a book as one could want on the subject of **The Police Procedural** (Bowling Green University Popular Press, cloth $20.95, paper $10.95). He is especially good on the origins of this sub-genre and the different types of policemen, e.g. "ethnic." His is a very accurate book, with one minor omission: while it is true that Lawrence Treat wrote Mitch Taylor "out" of his **novels**, he used him extensively in the long series of police procedural short stories he did for **EQMM**.

David Geherin's **John D. MacDonald** (Frederick Ungar, 250 Park

It's About Crime   24   Marvin Lachman

Ave. South, New York, NY 10003, cloth $11.95) is a fine survey of a very popular author's works. Geherin, an expert on the Private Eye, gives us a brief but comprehensive biography and captures very nicely the reasons behind JDM's success. But, really, Mr. G., Travis McGee's home, "The Busted Flush," is not as famous as 221 B Baker St.

For mystery film buffs, William Luhr's **Raymond Chandler and Film** (also from Ungar, no price on jacket) may be almost indispensable. It is the definitive book on the films made from Chandler's works as well as the films which Chandler worked on during his relatively short, unhappy career in Hollywood.

Two of the classic books about the mystery, **The Art of the Detective Story** (1946), edited by Howard Haycraft, and **The Detective Writer's Art** (1971), edited by Francis M. Nevins, Jr., contained scholarly yet entertaining essays. Last year saw the publication of two more fine collections of essays. Lucy Freeman edited **The Murder Mystique**, another Ungar book, and has gathered essays by eleven members of MWA. At least five--by Ed Hoch, Eleanor Sullivan, Shannon O'Cork, Franklin Lee Bandy, and D.R. Bensen--are gems. A good batting average and a good book.

H.R.F. Keating's **Whodunit: A Guide to Crime, Suspense and Spy Fiction** (Van Nostrand Reinhold, cloth $18.95) is not primarily a book of essays. However, it is the essays which rescue it from being one of the less useful reference books around. Two of the best are by Reginald Hill and Robert Barnard. Hill traces the historical growth from "the literature of crime" (e.g., DeFoe's **Moll Flanders**) to the **genre** of crime fiction. Barnard is excellent regarding the Golden Age in which there was an implicit contract between the author and the reader that the latter would be entertained by a problem appealing to the intellect. "If the reader guessed the solution he was pleased with himself; if he did not he was pleased with the author."

However, most of **Whodunit** is a replay of previous reference books in the field. The title is Ordean Hagen's. The biographies of detectives were done first, and in far greater numbers, in **Detectionary**. Finally, **Encyclopedia of Mystery and Detection** is light years ahead of this book in its biographies of authors. Included with the biographies in Keating's work is an almost incomprehensible system of evaluating some of the writer's work, based on rating characteristics like characterization, plot, readability, and tension by allotting a number of asterisks to each. Half-asterisk, I say about this system.

Two biographies appeared toward the end of 1982, and they are beauties. Roy Hoopes' **Cain** (Holt, Rinehart, and Winston, cloth $25.00) is likely to be the definitive work about this famous hard-boiled writer who didn't like to be thought of as "hard-boiled." Profusely illustrated, it contains 563 pages of text and over one hundred pages of sources, notes, and index.

Cain is so long because, especially during the early chapters, Hoopes chose not to be as selective as he might have been. Thus, we have some trivial reminiscences from Cain's childhood, e.g., the teacher who would not call him "Jamie", and the fact that he regretted all his life that his father had not vetoed his skipping from third to fifth grade because it placed him with fellow students who were older and more mature than he. If these incidents were traumatizing to Cain, Hoopes does not convince us.

Later, the abundance of detail is marvelous for the cumulative picture it gives us of the difficulties in "making it" as a writer. Incidentally, one of the actual pictures in this book, of Cain's friend and fellow writer, Morris Markey, is credited to none other than the creator of photographers Flash Casey and Kent Murdock: George

Harmon Coxe.

The only similarity between Cain and G.K. Chesterton is that in 1933 both were columnists for the Hearst press. GKC was the brilliant essayist and master of wit who created one of the most endurable detectives of all time, Father Brown. Alzina Stone Dale's biography, **The Outline of Sanity** (William B. Erdman, 255 Jefferson Ave., S.E., Grand Rapids, MI 49503, cloth $18.95), nicely balances its presentation of Chesterton as a man of letters and as a man of flesh and blood. It is not written especially for the mystery fan, but her subject's role in our genre is not neglected either. Dale is especially good on Chesterton's role in London's Detection Club.

I've made no secret of my love affair with San Francisco. When other commitments kept me from taking the official Dashiell Hammett tour during Bouchercon 1982, I did the walk on my own. I would recommend that any mystery fan who is in San Francisco try to hook up with Don Herron and spend what has been described to me as an enormously enjoyable couple of hours. Herron can be reached at 538 Jones St. #9207, San Francisco, CA 94102.

If you can't go there, you can still take the tour vicariously by purchasing **The Dashiell Hammett Tour** from Herron at the above address for $6.95. It contains photos, maps, bibliography, and the best capsule biography of Hammett I have ever read.

DEATH OF A MYSTERY WRITER

Dana Lyon at age 85 in Northern California in November 1982. She wrote **The Frightened Child** (1948), which was filmed in 1951 as **The House on Telegraph Hill** with Richard Basehart and Valentina Cortese. She also wrote seven other suspense novels, including **The Tentacles** (1950) and **The Lost One** (1958), the latter especially poignant and suspenseful. Occasionally, Dana Lyon wrote short stories, with "The Woman in the Stone House" (**EQMM**, May 1972) being an excellent example of her art.

Caryl Brahams at age 81 in London, December 4, 1982. She was a former dance critic who wrote books with a ballet background, including at least three mysteries: **A Bullet in the Ballet** (1937), **Casino for Sale** (U.S. title **Murder a la Stroganoff**), and **Six Curtains for Stroganova** (1945). She was best known to television watchers as the writer for the original British version of **That Was the Week that Was** in the early 1960s. More recently her name frequently appeared on public television in the U.S. as writer of a series of programs featuring the works of great lyricists like Lorenz Hart, Ira Gershwin, Johnny Mercer, et al. She collaborated on it and on at least six plays in the British theater with Ned Sherrin.

Audrey Roos at age 70 in Edgartown, Massachusetts, on December 11, 1982. With her husband, William E. Kelley, she wrote as Kelley Roos, creating the popular husband-and-wife detective team of Jeff and Haila Troy. They wrote eight novels about them, as well as several novelets, three of which were collected in **Triple Threat** (1949). "Two Over Par," a Troy short story, won fourth prize in **EQMM**'s 1949 contest. One of their non-series novels, **Scent of Mystery,** was a novelization of their 1959 film script. The film used a short-lived gimmicky process in which various smells were released in the theatre at appropriate moments in the action.

Audrey Boyers Walz at age 76 in Greenfield, Massachusetts, on February 14, 1983. As Francis Bonnamy she wrote eight novels about Peter Utley Shane as well as a short story, "The Loaded House," which won a prize in **EQMM**'s 1950 contest. Mrs. Walz also wrote two historical novels, **The Bizarre Sisters** and **The Undiscovered Country**. She was married to Jay Walz, long-time foreign correspondent for the New York **Times**. Together they wrote **Portrait of Canada**, a book based on their study of that country during his tour of duty in Ottawa from 1964 to 1973.

[Continued from page 12]
occasion of Wolfe's leaving the house--to attend an orchid exhibition or a gourmet dinner, as in one of his master works, **Too Many Cooks**, where Wolfe is guest of honor at an elite gathering of international master cooks. The greatest surprise, however, comes in **In the Best Families**, where the enemy is the impregnable and deadly Mafia bagman Arnold Zeck, who appears in earlier works, for example, with the consequence of a total bombing out of Wolfe's orchid greenhouse on the roof. In **In the Best Families** Wolfe leaves without a trace and does not return for six months, after he has lost 50 kg and has become completely unrecognizable, even to Archie--after which he can infiltrate Zeck's organization and stage his liquidation.

The portrayal of Wolfe, in general, is stamped with an almost intolerable chauvinism and a boundless conservative snobbery, but it should be obvious from what I have said above that I find the books inexpressibly charming. As is usual with art and culture, the style and the manner, rather than the message, impel the work. If one reads too many of the novels in a short time, they tend to become undistinguishable one from another; on the other hand, a single book every three or four months is comfortable, relaxing reading for me. As Archie Goodwin has established again and again, the way of genius is inscrutable, and a well-told story is not to be sneezed at. Therefore, I continue to return to the world of Nero Wolfe. This will make Archie happy, but will hardly amaze him.

[Continued from page 18]
seems to be a logical choice for an "ordinary" man, but to fireside adventurers, it's pretty impressive, pretty unusual. Perhaps this trip set the mode for the author's habit of transforming possible handicaps, such as the lack of a formal education, into advantages, for certainly travel and self-education (he reads about a book a day, now mostly technical works) have been central to his adult life and to his career: "The origin of the writing impulse is to read. You read, you read, you read!" And the process is still moving along at a brisk, productive rate. Bagley's readers will be pleased to hear that he has no intention to stop reading and writing. When asked what satisfaction writing gives him, he replied with a typical blend of humor and commitment:

> Well, let me say I write books because I don't know anything else to do. It's the only thing I'm qualified for, and I'm too old to go back to earning an honest living!
>
> And I am a writer. I was writing for many, many years before I made a success of it, and I don't know anything else. I suppose that I could retire now, but what would I **do** with myself? All I know is writing, you see--so I'll just carry on.

REEL MURDERS

MOVIE REVIEWS by Walter Albert

DAMSELS IN DISTRESS

I must admit that I have never been fond of those damsel-in-distress films in which an anxious heroine (her brow is usually creased), married to a homicidal maniac, is so enamoured of her prospective murderer that she can't bear to take the most elementary precautions to protect herself. A typical example of this **genus horribilis** is **Julie** (1956), starring Doris Day, Louis Jourdan, and Barry Sullivan. Day plays an airline stewardess who loses her bearings when she's on the ground and marries handsome psycho Jourdan after her first husband dies under circumstances which are only mysterious to her. Barry Sullivan plays the attentive other man hovering protectively around Julie with little success in persuading her that her husband is up to no good, again. Eventually, Julie is alone in an apartment to which Jourdan has traced her and when I went downstairs to breakfast she was pacing nervously while the camera cut frequently to shots of Jourdan closing in. When I returned, to my surprise I found that Julie, with grim but plucky determination, was attempting to land a very large plane. The pilot was nowhere to be seen, the co-pilot kept lapsing into a coma from which an attentive man (not Barry Sullivan) kept reviving him, and a phalanx of air controllers was giving landing directions from the flight tower of an airport which she was probably in imminent danger of demolishing. In line with my policy of not revealing endings, I will draw a discreet curtain over the remaining action.

One of the things that has always struck me in the classic DID films is the almost total absence of women other than the star. DIDs attract either psychos or **sympas** but never, or almost never, another woman. However, the revolution in social roles has not gone unnoticed by filmmakers, and a recent example of the DID film reflects some of the changes. **Without a Trace**, a film version of Bess Gutcheon's **Still Missing**, based on the real-life story of the still unsolved disappearance of a six-year-old boy on his way to school, was promoted by our local critics as an entertaining, well-made film. In the face of overwhelming apathy, the film was held over for two or three desultory weeks and then shunted off to the Regency Square, where I saw it on a Friday night with a substantial family audience.

Without a Trace stars British actress Kate Nelligan (who earned her credentials as a DID specialist in **Eye of the Needle** and Judd Hirsch, playing the police lieutenant who's put in charge of the investigation when Nelligan reports her son missing. As we were asked to believe that stewardess Day could be prompted into landing a plane, so are we asked to believe that Nelligan is a university English professor who teaches a course in modern poetry in which she lectures to a sizeable audience of over-age actors in the kind of ampitheater that in my part of the university world is only used for science courses. (Does anyone in Hollywood have any idea what has happened to registration in literature courses in the past decade?) My wife pointed out to me that the quote attributed, during a lecture on Robert Frost, to Pope was actually from Emerson, but I found the slip (for which we should really hold the screenwriter responsible) engaging and a reminder that no film based on "real life" is real and that a British actress posing as a professor of American literature in an American university is, after all, only playing. (The British usually are much better at playing Germans than they are at playing Americans. The current PBS series, **Private Schulz**, presents a Germany completely inhabited by British accents. I'm looking forward to the episode in which Private Schulz, "disguised" as an Englishman, is set down in wartime England where he must play a German impersonating an Englishman. The dilemmas posed for the hapless English actor are mind-boggling.)

In **Without a Trace**, Nelligan has a mother, a best friend, and some sympathetic women neighbors, but, true to the demands of the DID film, she is abandoned by all of them, and at the moment of crisis she is alone, without even the male policeman apparently willing to listen to her. And it is at this moment, when everything seems hopeless and she's almost ready to give up, that a **deus ex machina** is introduced to turn the situation around. And, since these are the eighties, the **deus** is a **dea**. In the Doris Day films, Doris hung in until the very end, and, although the men are, at times, almost literally propping her up to get her out of the Perilous Predicament, the Star is always center stage. In this example of female New Cinema, the star is allowed to go off-stage during the climactic chase. This permits the Inferior Male (Hirsch) to redeem himself but also involves one of the most unlikely coincidences ("Daddy, let's go to the park") and extreme double-takes that I've suffered through since the days of the Monogram serials. Nelligan is attractive and probably intelligent, and Hirsch is fine, but this DID variation finally succumbs to the same weakness that plagued the romantic DID vehicles: implausibility. And the virtues of **Without a Trace**--the good cast, fine photography, and tragic but not unusual situation--only serve, finally, to expose rather conceal the threadbare plotting.

Now that I have disposed of the romantic and realistic DID films, honesty obliges me to admit that there is one kind of DID film that I find not unappealing--the bizarre or the erotic. A late-night film I saw recently qualifies on both counts. **Lemora, Lady Dracula** (1973) is described in John Stanley's **Creature Features Movie Guide** (privately printed, 1981) as an "offbeat, surrealistic vampire flick with heavy artistic overtones," a fairly accurate, bite-sized summary. The basic narrative concerns an adolescent girl who has been redeemed by a fundamentalist congregation from her worthless parents and trained as a singer to witness for the church. When she receives word that her father is dying and would like to see her, she runs away, travelling through a nightmare country inhabited by prostitutes and lascivious rustics until she is waylaid and carried off by monstrous, semi-human creatures looking like rejects from Dr. Moreau's laboratory. Escaping from the stone prison they lock her into, she is "rescued" by a tall, beautiful woman dressed in black with thick white makeup and given a robe to put on for a mysterious ceremony. Both Lemora and the fey children who attend her are vampires, and the girl's father has become one of the Moreau-like creatures who had kidnapped her. The rest of the film is taken up with the girl's flight from Lemora and her cohorts and the vampire's eventual victory.

The film's colors are predominantly black and red with glossy highlights, and there is a veneer of seductiveness and erotic titillation in almost every frame. (Even in the opening sequences in the church, the girl is dominated by a young, intense minister of whom we are immediately suspicious.) The depiction of the vampire children is particularly effective, a blend of the diabolic and the pathetic. Lemora, who seems to be an untrained actress and reads her lines stagily (she is better at leering than reading) is the Dark Lady of romantic legend and exudes a sensual quality that gives the film a rather lurid cast. There is increasingly less distinction between the present and past, fantasy and reality, and the girl's flight from seduction becomes a sexual odyssey that is often quite disturbing.

Although **Lemora** is clearly an exploitation film and sometimes borders on the ludicrous, its implicit content pre-dates the recent rash of summer-camp psycho films but, like them, charts adolescents' ambivalent sexual feelings. The most common situation is one in which young girls or women are pursued by murderous/sexually threatening men or women. The ambivalence of the spectator's feelings toward the monster in the classic horror film (both admiration and fear) is exploited in a more troubling way. The classic film monster was often a tormented being with some impulse toward good; now, he--or she--is as threatening as the unspecified taboos and mysteries of sex, a disquieting visualization of the adolescents' deepest fears and instincts. The hulking, grotesquely masked demon of **Halloween** or the unseen avenger of **Friday the 13th**, as well as the mindless, bloody creature of **The Texas Chainsaw Massacre**, all seem to be drawn toward pubescent girls or toward couples, and there is more than a suggestion that sex is inherently evil and will be mercilessly punished. Mutilation is a standard element, and fears that the violence in these films will provoke similar attacks is a commonplace of some criticism. It's possible that the frenzied, bloody murders will excite some viewers, but it may be that the ways in which younger viewers' sexual fears are confirmed will be a more damaging effect of the violence. In the absence of clinical studies, such speculation cannot be confirmed, but it is clear that one result of the so-called sexual revolution has not necessarily been to make people less fearful of sexual relationships.

Another feature of these films is that very often the monster is not exorcised or destroyed. He lives again to spread havoc through one or more sequels. This was also true of the Universal Studio horror cycle, but there was usually some escape from the threat posed by the monster. In this open-ended narrative one can see a reflection of the contemporary fondness for unresolved plots. One of the attractions of genre has always been its sense of working through formulas of conflict and antagonism to a resolution or cartharsis. At the same time, critics have often perceived genre limitations to be its adherence to patterns and conventions and its opposition to the openness and flexibility of life to which "great" art is presumed to be more responsive. Like the anti-detective novel, where the narrative gaps are left unresolved, the conventions of the horror film seem increasingly to function not to quiet anxieties but to intensify them and may reflect a fairly general feeling that there are no longer satisfactory solutions to any problems. It may be a symptom of the disappearance of some of the traditional distinctions between elitist and popular art that popular art can feed contemporary anxieties, but that phenomenon, in itself, may be as disquieting as the fears it no longer mediates but intensifies.

The Reference Shelf

William Luhr. **Raymond Chandler and Film**. Frederick Ungar, 1982, ix-xv + 208 pp., bibliography and index, photographs, filmography, $7.95.

Al Clark. **Raymond Chandler in Hollywood**. Proteus, 1983, index, filmography, $11.95.

    I have paper editions of both these books: the Luhr is a 5-1/2 x 8" yellowback, the cover sporting a portrait of Chandler set into an oval frame next to a pulp illustration; the Clark is a large-sized 8 x 10-3/4" book, the cover featuring a brown hat with a revolver resting on the brim. The Luhr pages are densely packed with text in small type, while the Clark is profusely illustrated with stills, lobbycards and other advertising material for the films. Luhr is an associate professor of English and film at St. Peter's College, and Al Clark is a Spanish-born publicist and magazine editor who is currently creative director of the Virgin Records group, based in London. The copy for Clark's biography is probably written by him and is a tongue-in-cheek view of his life; Luhr's credentials are presented soberly. The casual reader is likely to assume that Luhr is writing a serious study of Raymond Chandler's Hollywood career and that Clark has put together an album for the film buff.

    In fact, both books are valid contributions to the literature on Chandler's Hollywood years. Luhr's approach is largely analytical, a close reading of his films. Clark went to Los Angeles where he interviewed people involved in the films and people who knew Chandler, and his narrative is a mixture of production information and film analysis. Clark unfortunately only cites his sources in his preface: there are neither notes nor bibliography. He seems more sensitive than Luhr to information furnished by people like Leigh Brackett, but both men communicate their enjoyment of the films and of Chandler's fictional world, and I would not want to be without either book. The layout on the Clark book is handsome, and the stills, not the tiny postage stamps one often sees, are generously displayed in an attractive format. I compared the two accounts of **The Long Goodbye** and while they are not perfectly congruent they are in general agreement, with, as one would expect, Luhr going into greater detail about the film and Clark more enlightening on the actual production. He incorporates a lengthy interview with Nina Van Pallandt into the chapter, and it is the insight furnished into the making of the film that makes **Raymond Chandler in Hollywood** a more intimate look at the Raymond Chandler film world.

[Continued from page 21]

    The fact that Kurland's third book is scheduled for upcoming publication means that, although we are out of the boom years, interest in the further doings of Mr. Sherlock Holmes and his associates remains high. It is up to future authors to preserve the high standards of Nicholas Meyer, John Gardner, and, of course, Sir Arthur Conan Doyle.

VERDICTS
Book Reviews

Donald Spoto. **The Dark Side of Genius: The Life of Alfred Hitchcock.** Little, Brown, 1983, 594 pp., $20.00.

He fooled us just as thoroughly as he scared us. Until his death three years ago, Alfred Hitchcock carefully cultivated the public image of his films as commercial suspense thrillers and of his private life as a model of bourgeois stolidity. In the late 1950s critics began taking his movies seriously and discovering the profound artistry beneath the cinematic technique. And now that he's dead the night side of the man, the sexual and psychological conflicts that tore him apart and gave rise to the tortured vision of his films, has surfaced into public view. Donald Spoto, whose **Art of Alfred Hitchcock** (1976) is by far the best critical study of its subject, has now written the fullest biographical study as well.

The crucial events in the director's life came early. His father was a cold, forbidding, Cockney greengrocer who, in Hitchcock's often repeated but unverifiable anecdote, had the five-year-old Alfred thrown in jail by a friendly constable for no apparent reason. His equally strange mother often made him stand by her bedside and tell her everything he did that day in intimate detail. He was subjected to a Catholic upbringing in which children were systematically terrorized with fear of death and eternal damnation and, perhaps worst of all, with fear and contempt for their own burgeoning sexuality. All these seeds fell on fertile ground. Even as a child, Hitchcock saw the world as a radically insecure place that could crash down around him at any moment. From an early age he was tormented by the inevitability of his own death. He stuffed himself with food to ward off insecurity and the powerful sexual desires and curiosities that he'd been taught to loathe, and he succeeded only in arousing repulsion in the women he now perversely wanted more than ever. His disgust at his own body and its appetites triggered a permanent psychological confusion, so that, in his thoughts and words, and symbolically in his films, eating and vomiting and defecation and sexual love and sadistic humiliation and rape became all but indistinguishable. This apparently remote and emotionless man was so consumed by terrors that he needed to compensate by exerting total control over his external environment and his movies--and by dominating, manipulating, degrading, bullying, and exploiting most of the people around him. At odd moments he could treat others with decency and even generosity, and his mousy wisp of a wife ruled the roost during their near-celibate fifty-five-year marriage. These relationships were the exceptions.

Much of Spoto's biography is a sober and thoroughly researched account of the facts of Hitchcock's public life and the circumstances surrounding the making of each of his films. But the leitmotif that gains in strength as Hitchcock ages is his grotesque inner life. He was a man attracted and repulsed by the same desires, and he made it impossible for others to give him the love that he longed for yet couldn't give himself. With consummate skill Spoto shows how the worst aspects of his character permeate his best films. **Notorious:** Claude Rains as an ugly little Fascist with a browbeating mother and romantic yearnings for Ingrid Bergman; Cary Grant as a man who expresses his unspoken love for Bergman by psychologically degrading her and forcing her to give herself to Rains. **The Wrong Man:** Henry Fonda victimized by a system that can destroy a person for no reason at any moment. **Vertigo:** James Stewart insanely remolding Kim Novak into his romantic image of lost love. **Psycho:** Tony Perkins as a mother-fixated mass murderer of women, gifted with the bleakest of insights into the human condition. These themes from deep in Hitchcock's soul form the subtexts of his most powerful pictures, and Spoto suggests that without them his films would just have been technical exercises in suspense. He and those around him paid the price for his art in the sufferings he endured and inflicted.

If he hadn't also been a visual genius, if he'd been unable to embody his terrors and desires and repulsions in film, he might have become one of the century's most hideous criminals. He seems to have made a star out of the previously unknown Tippi Hedren for the sole purpose of forcing her into his bed. When she refused, he subjected her during the filming of **The Birds** to a week-long quasi-sexual assault that brought her to the brink of collapse. Then he cast her in **Marnie** as a frigid thief who's raped by Sean Connery, but more or less consciously sabotaged the picture and ruined her acting career. His later **Frenzy** hinges on the most brutal rape-murder sequence in any Hitchcock film, although it might have been topped by a parallel scene in **The Short Night**, which he was preparing for the screen in his last months. In the end, when he knew that he'd never experience his ideal of love, his drinking and sexual harrassment of women employees intensified, and tears streamed down his face when on his deathbed he told Ingrid Bergman of his terror before the specter.

"I think that we're all in our private traps," Hitchcock's Norman Bates says in **Psycho**. "And none of us can ever get out. We scratch and claw, but only at the air, only at each other, and for all of it we never budge an inch." "Sometimes we deliberately step into those traps," replies the woman he will soon slash to death. "I was born in mine," he says. Perhaps Hitchcock, too, that brilliant and dreadful man, was born in his. Thanks to Spoto's compelling biography, whenever we see his films again we'll remember the wretched life that spawned them, and shudder. (Francis M. Nevins, Jr.)

Nathan Aldyne. **Cobalt.** Avon, 1982.

Dan Valentine's second case takes him to Provincetown for the hot summer tourist season. He talks comrade Clarisse Lovelace into joining him, sharing an apartment in Clarisse's uncle's house. She arrives to find everyone preparing for a gala costume party, with P'town's gay community in an uproar about who will be there with whom. Sure enough, there are several clashes and confrontations through the evening, and early in the morning Clarisse finds a body on the beach.

Although it is fascinating in its way, Aldyne has not produced here the success he had with **Vermillion**. Perhaps he'll do better with the upcoming **Slate**. Clarisse has taken over as the most sympathetic character, yet Valentine is the alleged detective. In fact, there is hardly any detection at all, just a lot of muddling around among the friends and suspects until the killer turns up. Valentine doesn't really come alive this time. In his concern to portray the composite of gay life and relationships, Aldyne neglected to make Valentine human. Ironically, that gay mileau is effectively drawn, but the people who inhabit it are shallow cardboard. Plot and characterization suffer in the interest of atmosphere and setting. While not the best of the year, it is far from the worst. (Fred Dueren)

Isaac Asimov, Charles G. Waugh, and Martin Harry Greenberg, editors. **Tantalizing Locked Room Stories.** Walker, 1982.

One strong testimony to the versatility of the mystery story lies in the fact that, regardless of all the new developments during the past couple of generations, the locked room story, the oldest and also the most tightly disciplined type of detective fiction, is still one of the most popular.

This collection of a dozen stories is arranged in chronological order, beginning with the three acknowledged classics of the type: Poe's "Murders in the Rue Morgue," Conan Doyle's "Adventure of the Speckled Band," and Futrelle's "Problem of Cell 13." The remaining nine cover a time span from a 1930 story by MacKinlay Kantor to one by Bill Pronzini and Michael Kurland published in 1976.

Asimov's brief introduction is disappointingly inadequate for a collection of this kind. For some reason, he has chosen to deal only incidentally with the locked room tale and has instead devised a broad discussion of puzzles and puzzle-stories generally. What is needed to introduce such a collection as this is one of two kinds of explanation, if not both. The mystery addict who loves a puzzle but is not familiar with the special formal limitations imposed on the locked room story needs an introduction to this type of tale, with an explanation of the locked room formula and how it works. The connoisseur, familiar with the hundreds of stories that have appeared in print, would appreciate a statement of the policy the editors followed in making the selection they offer here; the experienced reader will probably understand the reason for the inclusion of Cornell Woolrich's story, "Murder at the Automat," in which the murder-site is not really physically "locked," but he might like to know the basis for the use of the Jack Woodhams story, which is a locked room tale only by an extraordinary stretch of definition. Unfortunately, Asimov in his introduction does not address either of these readers' questions.

Reading a locked room story most closely parallels the experience of watching a magician perform an act. The writer first takes us on a tour of the "locked" area, showing us how carefully the windows and doors are sealed and eliminating all possibility of trapdoors and sliding partitions. Or, he may not confine his site to a physically enclosed area, choosing rather an open space which is nevertheless under such close observation that it hypothetically qualifies as "locked." Next he sets the temporal limits, demonstrating how, on the front end of the time-frame, no crime has been committed when the area is sealed, and how, at the conclusion of the period, the impossible deed has been done before the locked room is opened. If the crime is murder, our author may supply an added fillip by removing the weapon from the scene, thus deepening the mystery by eliminating the possibility of suicide. What our locked room author has done, in short, is to show us that the impossible crime has been committed. This out of the way, he proceeds to cheat.

We, of course, expect him to cheat, and the pleasure of the locked room story is proportional to the skill and flourish with which he does so. We know that it is impossible to pull rabbits out of an empty hat, and we honestly do not expect miracles to be performed or the laws of nature to be reversed. What we do want is to be amusingly conned. What we do not want is for our magician-author, having failed at producing rabbits, to conclude his act with a whimsical little homily about how God could have done it--which is literally what happens at the end of one of the stories in this collection.

There are two ways of cheating in the locked room story, which is the same thing as saying that there are two kinds of solutions to the impossible problem. One is the mechanical solution, the circumstance in which the room was not really "locked" to begin with, as is the case with "The Rue Morgue," "The Speckled Band," and "The Problem of Cell 13." The other solution consists in a violation of the time-frame: the crime had already been committed when the room was locked (as in two of S.S. Van Dine's novels), or it was not committed until after it was unlocked (as in Israel Zangwill's celebrated story, **The Big Bow Mystery**.) Both types of solutions--mechanical and temporal--are frequently used in all sorts of locked room stories, but for some reason the editors of the present collection have confined their selections to a single type, the mechanical.

Comparison is inevitable with the standard anthology, **The Locked Room Reader**, edited by Hans Santesson and published in 1968, and the comparison is decidedly unfavorable to the present collection. Why, with the abundance of good material to choose from, did the editors select these stories? Two of them (the one by Barry Perowne and the one by Robert Arthur) are based on the same concept; it is a clever enough idea, but surely the duplication was avoidable. The Perowne piece, as a matter of fact, is not a locked room story itself, but a story about a locked room story. The selection from Edward D. Hoch has a solution that is decidedly on the gimmicky side; Hoch can do much better with a locked room tale, as he did with "The Problem of the Octagon Room," one of his Dr. Sam Hawthorne stories published about a year and a half ago.

The last story in the collection, though, "Vanishing Act" by Bill pronzini and Michael Kurland, is a happy choice, based on a clever idea and a real credit to the locked room class. (George N. Dove)

Anne Morice. **Sleep of Death**. London: MacMillan, 1982; New York: St. Martin's, 1983, 176 pp.

This novel is Anne Morice's seventeenth mystery in the Tessa Crichton series in which Tessa is a professional actress and an amateur sleuth. This latest novel presents a situation similar to that in P.D. James's recent work, **The Skull Beneath the Skin**. Someone with a penchant for Shakespeare quotations is sending poison-pen letters to the already paranoid wife of a just-beyond-famous actor. (In James's novel, the recipient is a just-beyond-famous actress herself.)

Tessa has known the old actor from her childhood. Somewhat to her embarrassment, she is currently sharing the stage with him (he keeps falling asleep during rehearsals) and so is the perfect person to try to make sense of the death threats against his wife.

Morice always gives special attention to character development, and she draws the characters in this novel skillfully. All the characters in the closed circle of suspects are reasonably deserving of suspicion, and indeed one of them is guilty. The interrelationships of the cast, the management, and some of the close friends and lovers make Tessa's job more challenging and the plot believable.

Morice uses an old device at the end of the novel. After confessing all to a person with no legal authority (in this case, Tessa, of course), the murderer nobly commits suicide. This ending fits Morice's and the genre's demand for restitution while not requiring any of the messy details of trial and punishment at society's expense.

Sleep of Death is Morice's best since **Death in the Round**. Theater buffs will like the theatrical atmosphere, and other detective fiction fans will like the neatly crafted plot. (Martha Alderson)

David Beaty. **Cone of Silence**. Pan Books, 1960, 254 pp. First published by Secker & Warburg, 1959.
Nevil Shute. **No Highway**. Pan Books, 1963, 281pp. First published by Heinemann, 1948.

In **TMF** 7:1:32, Marvin Lachman observed that British writers leave their American colleagues behind when it comes to quality spy novels. This is probably all the more so when it comes to mystery/adventure tales involving technical or exotic backgrounds. One of the backgrounds which is **inherently** technical, as well as suspenseful, is aeronautics. In **Cone of Silence** and **No Highway** this suspenseful background is exploited in two different ways, from two different viewpoints: from that of the pilot who flies the planes, and that of the engineer who researchers their designs.

Author David Beaty served as an RAF squadron leader in World War II and then as a civilian BOAC pilot. Later he took to writing novels with aviation backgrounds which straddle the border between crime fiction and dramatic adventure fiction, such as **Heart of the Storm** (1954), **The Proving Flight** (1956), **Sword of Honor** (1965), and **Cone of Silence**. It could be argued that the latter is not a crime novel, since no crime occurs in it. On the other hand, however, there is courtroom action, excitement, in-flight suspense, mass death, detection, and a surprisingly clever solution.

The new Phoenix planes are the pride of England's aeronautical engineers. The planes are also the first British **jet** airliners, operated by British Empire Airways. The book opens with a court inquiry into a recent Phoenix accident. In Ranjibad, Pakistan, upon trying to take off, Captain George Gort ran out of airstrip before getting the plane off the ground, and crashed. No one was hurt, but Gort was blamed. Pilot error was the verdict of the inquiry. There were witnesses at Ranjibad who maintained that Gort always pulled the nose of the plane up too high too soon, making it harder to lift off at the proper time. Gort claims, however, that he did nothing wrong, that he flew by the book. But later he has another accident, suspiciously similar, and the consequences are much more serious. No one else has had such accidents. Why only Gort? Some think he is getting too old. Hugh Dallas, the Airways' training captain, is not satisfied with the decisions against Gort, so he investigates the accidents. Gort always flies by the book, so "pilot error" seems unlikely.

Dallas's investigation into the causes of the accidents comes very close to being fair-play detection and involves physical clues based on aeronautics as well as clues based on character. The solution is totally unexpected, logical, cogent, and realistic. It is sort of an "invisible hand" solution which is almost clever enough to stand up to the best of Golden Age puzzle-play. Besides these virtues, the book gives an intriguing picture of young postwar Britain's optimistic emergence into the jet age.

Because of the aviation backgrounds, the books of Beaty are sometimes compared to those of Nevil Shute. Like Beaty, Shute has technical experience which informs many of his books. He was an aeronautical calculator and engineer throughout the 1920s, and both early books (**Mazaran**, 1926) and later ones (e.g., **The Rainbow and the Rose**, 1958) involve aviation. Perhaps critics were thinking of **No Highway** as the point of comparison between the two authors. Although it too is arguably not a crime novel, it does have suspense and mild detection woven into a background of high drama.

The Reindeer are Britain's newest pre-jet airliners, and narrator Dr. Dennis Scott of the Royal Aircraft Establishment is in charge of a research staff to see that all goes well with them. However, one of Scott's staff, a cranky introverted genius named Honey, has a theory that the planes are unsafe, that their tails are due to go brittle and collapse after 1440 hours of flight. No one believes Honey, for he is also known to study Pyramidology and other paraphenomena. The trouble is, no one can check his theory, because it is based on the mathematics of the infant science of nuclear physics, which Honey understands better than anyone else in England. In order that Scott confirm Honey's theory, Honey is sent to Canada to investigate a Reindeer accident which had been chalked up to pilot error. But there are doubts. Did the tail break? Complications arise when, on the way across the Atlantic, Honey learns that the plane he is flying in is a Reindeer which has flown just about 1440 hours.

The detection in the story is carried out by Scott. Is Honey correct about the tails? Are the planes dangerous? Should they all be grounded? Since the answers are urgent and since Scott cannot understand Honey's theory, he seeks to confirm or refute it by trying to understand the man himself. He digs into Honey's character and zanily recondite hobbies. As detection it is mild, but interesting in spots, and it leads to a satisfying conclusion.

Shute is clearly the better writer, and he does an excellent job of explaining technicalities without condescending. He makes the crystallization of tale plane spars actually interesting. In contrast, much of Beaty's technical terminology remains unexplained, including the exact meaning of the title, which became a gag in the **Get Smart** series. Although **No Highway** preceeds **Cone of Silence** by eleven years and deals with propeller craft, there are many similarities, from the shiny new airliner models to the accident investigations and in-flight suspense. It is also curious to note that the Pan reprintings of the books are only three years apart, and, although no jet figures in **No Highway**, by its third printing, 1965 (well into the jet age), the Peyton Place style cover shows the characters bunched together in front of a jet. (Greg Goode)

Armin Arnold and Josef Schmidt. **Reclams Kriminalromanführer.** Stuttgart: Reclam, 1978, 455 pp.

Part of German publisher Reclam's well-known Führer (guidebook) series on aspects of the arts and culture, this is a historical, encyclopedic, bibliographical, and critical overview of crime fiction (almost) the world over. Compiled by two German professors at McGill University, it is divided into three main sections. The first section (pp. 7-44) includes historical material such as an essay on the development of the genre which includes elements as diverse as Biblical crime, ancient Chinese detective fiction, and dime novels—as well as a timetable of the most important dates in the history of the genre. The second section (pp. 45-362) is set up like **Encyclopedia of Mystery and Detection** but without illustrations, filmographies or character entries. Under authors' bylines or most familiar names is to be found biographical, bibliographical, and critical information, and, frequently, plot summaries of noteworthy novels. The third section (pp. 363-455) includes expository and critical essays by various writers on crime fiction in world literature (Arabia, China, Germany, Italy, Japan, Russia, Scandinavia, Spain and Latin America, and West Africa), appended to which in several cases are bibliographies of secondary sources. The third section also contains a list of one hundred important crime novels, a character index featuring more than eight hundred detectives and criminals, a bibliography of secondary sources, and an author index.

The authors are thoroughly familiar with the standard English-language critical material, including **The Armchair Detective**, and references to sources in German, French, Spanish, Italian, and Swedish also can be found. Heavy but acknowledged use throughout is made of Ordean Hagen's **Who Done It?**, **Encyclopedia of Mystery and Detection**, and **A Catalogue of Crime**. Especially interesting for readers familiar with English-language crime fiction and secondary sources is the wealth of information on non-Anglo-Saxon characters, such as Fantomas, and non-Anglo-Saxon authors, such as Johannes Mario Simmel or Adolf Muschg. There is also a somewhat unusually large or small emphasis placed on English-language authors—Donald McNutt Douglass is given much more space in the encyclopedia than William Campbell Gault, and authors such as Sinclair Gluck and Sidney Hobson Courtier are included. There is a great deal of information on English-language crime fiction that is not available in any of the standard critical works in English.

The errors seem to be mostly those of omission, and some of the sections are weaker than seems necessary. It is surprising, in a book that covers so many countries' contributions to world crime fiction, that no mention is made of the large number of crime novels being published in India. Also, none of the several bibliographies of secondary sources even scratches the surface of the mass of critical material on the ancient Chinese detective story. Finally some of the bio-bibliographical data on authors included in the encyclopedic section is sketchier than necessary. For example, it is overlooked that Robert Milward Kennedy is the pseudonym for two people, Milward Rodon Kennedy Burges and Archibald Gordon McDonell, and not just the former. Also, some thirty of George Robert Sims' novels are overlooked, it being misleadingly stated that he has at least three to his credit (p. 314). But all in all, **Reclams Kriminalromanführer** is perhaps the single best guide to crime fiction (almost) around the world. (Greg Goode)

Ted Sennett. **Masters of Menace: Greenstreet and Lorre.** E.P. Dutton, 1979, $8.95, softbound.

The Maltese Falcon was their first film collaboration, but it was far from their last. Through the years their films have been entertaining insomniacs, film cultists, and mystery fans alike. Now, in **Masters of Menace: Greenstreet and Lorre**, we have the perfect film-goer's companion to compliment these two fine character actors.

The book gives us the separate lives of Peter Lorre and Sidney Greenstreet. The films they made apart from each other and the films they did together. There is also a chapter covering the film **The Maltese Falcon**. All this information and material is arranged in a very understandable and readable order. The filmography of each actor is separate and contains each film's name, cast, date, and director.

At the back of the book is a very useful bibliography and index for the avid reference fan.

Do not expect the biographies on the two actors to be deeply personal. It just is not so, although they do a fair job of touching on most of the major points of the two actors' lives and definitely cover their careers.

The book is full of photographs of their movies along with some personal photos of Lorre and Greenstreet with various actors.

This is an entertaining book and well worth the money. For the collector's benefit, there is no hardcover edition. It is a paperback original (so stated on the back cover). (Randy Himmel)

Richard and Frances Lockridge. **Murder Comes First.** Pocket Books, 1982, 208 pp., $2.95.

There is simply no mistaking a Mr. & Mrs. North mystery novel, and it is great to have them back in print again. Why hasn't anybody thought of it sooner? The warm, comfortable sounds of their adventures together have been sorely missed.

In this one of two just reprinted by Pocket, three of Pam's maiden aunts from Cleveland have come to the big city for a visit. Disaster strikes when another friend they are calling on mysteriously dies of poison. While Pam's Aunt Thelma may be as unlikely a murder suspect as you can imagine, that doesn't stop Deputy Chief Inspector Artemus O'Malley from thinking he can wrap it up quickly.

The inspector, Bill Wiegand admits to Pam, likes things simple. Sergeant Mullins, of course, knows better. "I should have known," he says. "It's begun to go screwy."

Part of the screwiness is that the FBI eventually gets involved, for reasons somewhat pertinent to the date of the story [it was first published in 1951]. Even so, in spite of this worn-out bit of murkiness at the core, this is still as bright and irresistable a work of entertainment as it ever was.

More! [B] (Steve Lewis)

Virginia Rich. **The Cooking School Murders.** Dutton, 1982, 207 pp., $11.95.

For a nice, gently nostalgic Midwestern tale of murder that will remind you of nothing less than home-folks all the way through, look no further. (Of course, if you come from a long line of Manhattanites or native Californians, you may be left wondering what the charm of living in Iowa may actually be, even after reading this book, but then again, some people are beyond help.)

Seriously, though, as an amateur sleuth in this first of a new series, Mrs. Potter has the right idea. As a widow in her early sixties, she's seen enough of life to be convinced that when it comes to murder, an honest character study of the people involved will always prove to be an essential key to its solution. So do I (even though, of course, that's where any resemblance between Mrs. Potter and myself most definitely ends).

Three deaths occur the same evening in Harrington, Iowa, immediately after, it seems, the first meeting of an advanced cooking class offered by the local high school. One is that of a long-time friend of Mrs. Potter's--apparently a suicide. Another is that of the new **femme fatale** in town, whom blackmail seems to follow like a well-trained setter. She, obviously, has been murdered, and it comes as no great surprise, but the death of a naive young schoolmarm seems to have been purely an accident.

Everyone else takes the "obvious" answers to the questions raised by these three nearly coincident deaths. Not Mrs. Potter, however, who putters around and unknowingly puts her own life on the line as she busily constructs various scenarios for the crimes, placing each of her many friends and acquaintances into every possible role.

Naturally she fails to put the solution together quite correctly enough, until it is very nearly too late. I thought the final outcome rather unlikely myself, and, if you will, a bit of a let-down to a mystery novel that till then had me very nicely entertained.

So overall, I'd have to call this one a relative lightweight in the world of amateur detection, but it's also undeniably a mystery with its own built-in source of warmth and charm--just enough to ward off the ever-approaching chill of murder.

P.S.--If you are so inclined, you can skip the recipes. [B] (Steve Lewis)

A.C.H. Smith. **Extra Cover.** Wiedenfeld and Nicholson, 1981.

Charley Midsomer lives by his wits but they haven't been too sharp lately, and, to get some of his money back, his main creditor arranges a job for him. The job is for Charley to join a weekend house party and then to put the frighteners on a guest whom the party host will finger. Sounds simple enough, except that Charley knows that he's not as tough as people think him, he doesn't know who he's to intimidate, or why, and what their reaction will be. Reasonable little plot, but toward the end, when the complications inevitably multiply, it carries less conviction. One very nice thing about the book is the cricketing backdrop in front of which the play is set. The weekend guests all take part in a cricket match and Charley finds himself on the field pitting his wits (cricketing and otherwise) against the enemy. The author clearly knows his cricket, and American readers will have fun trying to piece together and interpret the cricketing lore revealed. "Extra cover" is, incidentally, a fielding position in right field but much closer to the bowler than right field would be to a baseball pitcher. (Bob Adey)

Friedrich Dürrenmatt. **The Judge and His Hangman.** Jenkins, 1954.

An odd short novel by a Swiss writer about a dying detective, Inspector Barlach, and his determination to bring to justice a criminal who has flaunted justice throughout Barlach's career. Like a lot of continental writing, this is more about mood than plot--but plot there nevertheless is, with a contrived, if guessable, twist in the tale. A change from the usual fare. (Bob Adey)

The Documents In the Case (Letters)

From Howard W. Sharpe, P.O. Box 204, St. Kilda, Victoria, AUSTRALIA 3182:

Thank you for **TMF** 7:1, received and read today. Of particular note is Bob Sampson's "Detection by Other Means"—If there were a bookshop here in Melbourne offering pulps, I would be there right now, searching for some of the items which Bob lists at the end of his article.
Last week I discovered **TMF** 6:2, which I had set aside after reading it last year in order to comment on two items on the last page.
In your editorial comments on Barry van Tilburg's letter you take up his reference to Howard Baker. The fact is that Baker was both author **and** publisher. Baker was at that time the proprietor of Mayflower Books, but eventually he began to use his name as publisher. Over many years I was in touch with him as a subscriber to a large series of facsimile editions of boys' magazines, which project is still progressing. He also published the final series of Sexton Blake stories, in paperback format--these would be known to many members of our circle.
The other item of interest to me was Barry's contemplation of continuing his noble series on spy stories by turning to paperbacks (my favourite article in every issue). Now God be praised! I see in **TMF** 7:1 (from a terse editorial comment) that he has not changed his mind. One has only to think of the Joe Gall, Sam Durell and Matt Helm series to realize how deserving the paperbacks are of such treatment. I am not forgetting the fine articles about them which we have already enjoyed in **TMF**. In fact, the book I am most desperate to obtain is not one of the aristocratic hardcovers, but Philip Atlee's paperback **The Makassar Strait Contract**. (If you ever hear of an available copy, I'll give you a spotter's fee!!)
It was nice to still have some Steve Lewis reviews. Boy, are we going to miss him!
[I'm afraid you are going to have to wait for a while for Barry's series on spy stories in paperback. When Barry proposed the series, I thought that he was nearing the end of his hardback series and that we could just take up with the paperbacks right away. As it happens, however, he still has quite a few hardback dossiers to get through, and, with space in these pages at a premium, I am unable to run the two series concurrently. I realize that this puts the spy fanatics among us

in an intolerable position—wanting the present series to go on for ever and yet wanting it to end so that the other series can begin—and for this I am sorry. [Ironically, Barry has not yet sent along the next hardback installment, so this issue of TMF is without either.]

As for The Makassar Strait Contract, I hope that some TMFer will have an extra copy on hand and will send it on to you without delay. Should that not happen, give me a nudge in about six months and I'll see what I can do. I think I have a copy packed away in one of about fifty boxes of books that I have in storage, and if I can find it it's yours as a gift.]

From Bob Randisi, 1811 East 35th St., Brooklyn, NY 11234:

This letter was prompted by Bob Adey's review of Timothy Harris's **Goodnight and Goodbye** in **TMF** 7:1, but I'll get to that later. First I'd like to say how much I liked the Brad Foster cover, and I hope to see more by him. He seems to have a way with women—on paper, anyway.

Can't say I particularly enjoyed the articles in this issue, with the possible exception of the **Black Mask** piece by E.R. Hagemann, but then I have much the same problem with **TAD**. As in the case of **TAD**, I find most of my enjoyment in the regular columns, reviews, and letter page.

Okay, so this brings us back to the Adey review. I enjoyed **Goodnight and Goodbye** very much, but I'm not writing to argue with his review. It was his comment about Kyd still being a "top ten" P.I. that prompted me to sit down and write immediately. (I only hope I mail it as fast.)

I'd like to offer a top ten P.I. list of my own, and, as wonderful as the "golden age" P.I.'s were--Marlowe, Spade, and Co.--you'll notice that my list is dominated by P.I.'s who appeared later on. The only limitation here is that each P.I. must have appeared at least twice. Here's the list:

> Bill Pronzini's "Nameless"
> Tucker Coe's Mitch Tobin
> Michael Collins' Dan Fortune
> Ralph Dennis's Jim Hardman
> Thomas B. Dewey's Mac
> Larry Block's Matt Scudder
> Richard Hoyt's John Denson
> Arthur Lyons' Jacob Asch
> Jonathan Valin's Harry Stoner
> (three-way tie for #10)
> Loren Estleman's Amos Walker
> Warwick Downing's Joe Reddman
> Marcia Muller's Sharon McCone

There you are, and the only "old" eye in the group is Mac. Of course, honorable mention would go to Marlowe, but Spade never was one of my favorite P.I.'s. Some one-shot (so far) P.I.'s with a shot at my top ten would be Jack Livingston's Joe Binney and Sara Paretsky's V.I. Warshawski.

Honorable mention for other P.I.'s who have appeared at least twice would go to Stephen Greenleaf's John Marshall Tanner, Timothy Harris's Thomas Kyd, Mark Sadler's Paul Shaw, and Joe Gores' DKA team.

I'm sure if I kept looking I could find a few more to mention, but I'm not going to. I might not stop.

And if anyone thinks that Parker's Spenser was an accidental oversight ... he wasn't!

From Philip T. Asdell, 5719 Jefferson Blvd., Frederick, MD 21701

I realize that an important function of "higher education" in our country is (along with athletics, the making of social contacts, and vocational training) to keep as many people as possible out of the labor force for as long as possible. I also realize that to keep so many people occupied it apparently is necessary to "offer" courses which do little to train or stretch minds. But, even so, when I read in publications for detective and mystery fiction enthusiasts that one or another institution of higher learning actually offers a course in that subject I am, in turn, amazed, dismayed, and bemused.

Glory be! To learn that a "credit" for the "study" of detective fiction is given equal weight with time spent studying U.S. constitutional history, Shakespeare, plant physiology, or the calculus boggles the mind!

The justification for "studying" detective fiction is, I have read, that such literature often reflects the social conditions of the time when it is written. Articles of this kind appearing in journals for enthusiasts most often mention in this connection, usually to the exclusion of others, the works of Messrs. Hammett and Chandler and their portrayals of the vibrant cultural life of southern California in the 1920s and 1930s. A conscientious social historian, when teaching a course in U.S. social history, might, in passing, mention to his students that the novels of these two gentlemen would make interesting spare-time reading. To manufacture a "course" out of their works and others in the field is to waste teachers' and students' limited times. It is also a waste of students', parents', and taxpayers' money.

Abraham Flexner, in his perceptive work, **Universities: American, English, German** (New York: Oxford University Press, 1930), deplored the degree-granting innovations called schools of business, home economics, journalism, hotel administration, etc. Since then a sort of Gresham's Law has really set in as more and more trifling courses are offered. One doesn't need much imagination to contemplate what Flexner would have to say about courses in detective fiction. Chandler himself once described our education as "a cultural flop." Perhaps the latest flap about the flop in the quality of our education will lead to a shake-out of courses in detective fiction and others before a large part of our educational system becomes a corpse.

From Virginia L. Struhsaker, 1217 W. Vine St., Stockton, CA 95203:

Enjoy magazine very much. Especially this issue's articles on Capt. J.T. Shaw's **Black Mask** and the Joe Orton and Tom Stoppard plays. Was just on a Reference Panel at the 1st Annual Mystery Writers Conference given at the University of the Pacific Campus sponsored by the Friends of the Stockton Public Library and the Associates of the University of Pacific Libraries (2-26-83). Reported on mystery magazines past and present, including **Black Mask** and **The Mystery Fancier**. Also recently saw Orton's **Loot**. S.F. ACT company usually do an Orton or a Stoppard play each year.

From Fred Isaac, 1685 San Lorenzo, Berkeley, CA 94707:

I'm just back from a day in Stockton, CA, where the University of the Pacific and the county public libraries held an all-day meeting entitled "Fog, Falcon, and Foul Play." Though I can't admit to having learned any new lore (except regarding the speakers), I did come away with added conviction that the genre is going in two directions.

Speakers for the morning session were Marcia Muller, Collin Wilcox, and Julie Smith (all writers) and Don Herron, whose specialty is Hammett lore. The best was Herron, whose knowledge of Bay Area-related mysteries is omniverous. The rest talked about their methods of writing, and their characters, and a bit about their methods of composition.

After lunch, each of them had an hour session with any of the crowd who wanted to see and talk to them. (I went with Wilcox, in part because I think Hastings is under-rated.) After that there was a session on "Mystery reference sources and specialized tools." And that was it. Obviously, I spoke to the people I knew (Bill Pronzini was there with Muller, and I saw other folks I met at last year's Bouchercon in S.F.) but not much more was substantive, or useful to me.

I don't know if you're going to the PCA in April, but if you are I'd like to see you. George Dove's panel on criticism (Saturday, 10:30-noon) should be an interesting forum, and I plan to set off some fireworks.

My premise is that those of us who wish to comment on the form in an analytic, formal, or academic way are placing a growing distance between ourselves and our fellow readers. It worries me that this is occurring. And on the other side, there are questions whether the mystery is accepted as "valid" among the rest of the academic community. I don't plan to answer the question, only to pose it. Even so, I hope to avoid a firestorm, or (as sometimes happens) the prospect of being ignored (the bringer of bad tidings, as it were).

TMF comes in because the woman speaking on magazines spoke of the magazine as "very scholarly," and disdained it as not for "average people." Grrrrr!! I plan to bring this up if I have the chance.

[So, how'd it go, Fred? George?]

From Bob Adey, 7 Highcroft Ave., Wordsley, Stourbridge, West Midlands, DY8 5LX, ENGLAND:

I was very pleased to receive **TMF** 7:1.[...] Very good lead articles. Fascinating insight into Captain Shaw's management of **Black Mask**. No wonder it was so successful.

I also thoroughly enjoyed Bob Sampson's rundown of the Semi-Dual series. I'm quite a sucker for detectives of the occult but had never heard of this particular series. Why on earth did no one put any of them between hard covers?

On the subject of occult detectives, I recently ran across an unusual investigator with leanings in that direction. The book is **Karl Grier** by Louis Tracy (Hodder and Stoughton, 1905 [not 1906 as Al Hubin had it], Clode, 1906. It's subtitled "The Strange Story of a Man with a Sixth Sense," and the first few chapters are, effectively, separate short stories in which the young Grier establishes his reputation as a clairvoyant, able to locate missing persons and forecast events. Grier is not really a detective in the pure sense of the word, but it does make for an interesting and unusual book--and one with a very attractive pictorial cover.

I hope that the game of cricket is now clear to you all and I enclose a review of a recent mystery with a strong cricketing background [A.C.H. Smith, **Extra Cover**].

From Ev Bleiler, who is still at large somewhere in New Jersey:

On that trail of peacock tracks and chewed-up feathers .... It was good to read Bob Adey's detailed description of what a cricket player really does. It clears up things.

I wouldn't dispute Bob's opinion that a good cricket player could throw a ball through a window opening about seventy feet away. I admitted that in my article, but qualified it by adding "though not unfailingly," as seems only reasonable. But even here, with a ball, the question is whether you would stake your life on it.

But what a good bowler can do with a ball on a cricket grounds is a little misleading, for Carr's situation is much more complex. Gardner was not throwing a ball, but a much heavier, strangely shaped, strangely balanced object, through a small space with very little clearance. And Gardner had a single-try situation. He could not retrieve the fallen gun if he missed (and, God knows, it probably would have gone off in midair) and try again. Visibility was poor, the distance was somewhat greater than that on a cricket grounds, and Gardner was not standing on an open field, but in a low-ceilinged room at a window with limited exit space.

This brings up the question of arm position again. It would seem obvious that any sort of cricket or baseball throw would not be optimal for him. Apart from a direct miss, what Gardner has to worry about is the gun's striking the window sill, frame, or sash because of imperfect clearance. The gun is fourteen inches long; the vertical window aperture is a maximum of sixteen inches, which means that if the gun approaches the window with its long axis completely vertical, if it is only one and one half inches off dead center, the trick will fail and Gardner will hang.

What this implies is that the vertical rotation of the gun in the air must be controlled. The horizontal rotation is much less important, since the window is four feet wide. Gardner's best bet is to make the gun rotate horizontally, and he can do this best by scaling or flipping the gun, giving it a horizontal rotation as it leaves his arm. Cricket and baseball are not likely to help here, but discus-throwing might.

Now, all this is argument up in the air, and I would suggest a practical application or experiment to see what would really happen. Why don't the readers of **TMF** make weighted models of the gun in question and throw them at their neighbors' windows? (I'll have to beg off, myself, since I can't hit a garage door with a ball.)

Or, better yet, maybe your British subscribers could pool their resources, hire Lords (if it is hireable), and engage the best cricketers to experiment for them. I can picture the scene-- the long line of bowlers, the glee or dismay at success or failure, the world's press standing agape in fascination, Carr's agent rubbing his hands together ....

But-- firm, secure knowledge!

Ola Strom's kind letter makes me want to reread **The Crooked Hinge**, which I remember as somewhat farfetched in solution. Also somewhat misleading about The Red Book of Appin. But Washington's Birthday is past.

For Mr. Strom's information, my **Guide to Supernatural Fiction** has been published and is available from Kent State University Press, Kent, Ohio. I would urge all your subscribers to buy copies, since I get royalties from it. It is a big book, fine for pressing flowers or hiding love letters. Or, since (squared off) it is roughly the same size and weight as Carr's outrageous pistol, it would be excellent for throwing through window openings.

As for **Before Poe**, I don't know. It needs extensive reresearching, revision, rewriting, and I don't know when or if I'll ever get to it.

From Linda Toole, 40 Hermitage Rd., Rochester, NY 14617

Nice scam you've got there. In November I get a letter purporting to be from a fellow subscriber commenting on something in **TMF 6:6. Of course** I haven't received it yet. My copy arrives 2-3 weeks after the letter. Funny thing, in that issue is an offer to subscribe to **TMF** 7 at either the old, slow second class rate or at the new, speedy, first class rate. When I wrote a panicky letter to you asking about 6:6 you stated my alleged correspondent received his magazine first class! Okay, you win, here's my check for the extra $3.00. How many other suckers bought it? [**Numbers don't matter, Linda; you'll always be my favorite sucker.**]

I'm glad Brad Foster signed on. He does great work. Steve Lewis will be missed.

Bob Sampson absolutely blew me away with "Maps of Xiccarph." I am just young enough to have missed the pulps, but Bob's article made me feel as though I was riding the bike and in Steve's Magazine Exchange. Talk about evocative! When is this man going to write a book?! [**He already has, twice that I know about, and several others are in the pipeline.** The Night Master, **a study of The Shadow, was published last year by Pulp Press at $14.95, and I mentioned it in "Mysteriously Speaking ...."** From what I hear, the second printing is already out of print, but you might drop Bob Weinberg a line to see if he has an odd copy left on his shelves. His address is 15145 Oxford Dr., Oak Forest, IL 60452. The first volume of Bob's multi-volume history of the pulps, Yesterday's Faces, is being published by The Popular Press (Bowling Green State University, Bowling Green, OH 43403); I recently received a catalogue from Bowling Green showing a 1982 publication date for it, but I don't believe it made it into print until earlier this year. I haven't seen a copy, and I've lost the damned catalogue so I can't tell you what the price is, but I'm sure it's a good value, whatever the cost. Bob just doesn't do bad work.]

May I use this space to publicly extract foot from mouth and mumble my apologies? The Wolfe Pack delivered three issues of **The Gazette** at the dinner in December. Good news and bad news for the **Bibliography.** Volume I is pretty much as represented (although I can't find Reis's "Footnote Written on a Rag"). Volume II shot you all to hell and back. First, it is Winter, 1983, not 1980. Second, I find very little correlation between the contents and the listings in the **Bibliography.** Live and learn, right? By the way, have you ever found anyone to take your money for a sub?

[**Last things first: Irving Kamil sent me a copy of a renewal form he had received, and I promptly filled it out and sent it in together with a check; so far, nothing. As for the conflicts between what is in** The Gazette **and what we said would be in it in our** Rex Stout: An Annotated Primary and Secondary Bibliography, **an explanation** is in order, particularly since the delinquency of the powers that be (or were) at The Gazette bids fair to make us look like a bunch of bungling bibliographers. What happened was this. One of my associates on the bibliography was, of course, John McAleer, who appears to be one of the few people on earth whose letters the original editor of The Gazette would answer. John did most of the work on the criticism section of the bibliography, and, when he obtained advance information about the contents of the next few issues of The Gazette we all agreed that, in the interest of completeness, they should be included in the bibliography, even though the issues in question were somewhat late getting into print. None of us had any idea just how late the damned things would be, and we certainly had no expectation that, having allowed us to cite the contents in our book, the powers that be (or were) would make what appear to be wholesale changes in the publication's contents. There's a lesson in this, and it hasn't been lost on me.]

I know that mystery encompasses many subgenres and that everyone is entitled to an opinion. I also appreciate negative reviews; they save me valuable time and money. But. What in the name of heaven was Mr. Wooster's review of **Hobgoblin** in 6:6! I can't believe that anyone enthusiastic and/or knowledgeable enough to subscribe to a mystery fanzine would ever mistake this book for a mystery. (Yes, I've read it.) The only reason Mr. Wooster seems to have for reviewing it is so he can sneer down his nose at it. What next--reviews of V.C. Andrews?

Am I the only subscriber who reads less than a thousand words a minute? Time after time I read (in a letter or a review) that a book was a "pleasant evening's" or "a few hours'" entertainment. I'm considered a fairly rapid--to say nothing of tenacious/voracious--reader, but I find these claims rather fantastic. Come on, confess. Nero Wolfe is a slow reader, and we all know how bright he is! [There was a brief period, immediately after I graduated from college the first time, when I would watch TV all night until the test pattern came on immediately after the post-midnight rerun of Peter Gunn and then read two books before going to bed. Honest. That day is long past, however. Nowadays, if I watch more than half an hour of prime-time TV at one sitting I feel as though my brain is turning to jello. Worse than that, though, is the fact that I've completely lost the ability to read quickly. It's a very short book indeed that I manage to read in a single sitting, even if I start immediately after supper and continue on until midnight. I'm getting old. Another decade and I'll be unable to finish the comic strips in a single evening.]

In reply to a letter in Volume I you stated that you have never seen a Nero Wolfe movie on TV. I'm sure you know by now that Stout was less than delighted with the movies and stipulated in his contracts that they never be shown on TV.

Since my last letter I've acquired several Keeler books. I'm waiting for a relatively uninterrupted stretch of time in which to read one (or more). Somehow I get the impression that the books can't be read during commercial breaks on TV. Don't worry about me, Guy. I've got a large ball of twine and a good compass. [**Don't forget the dramamine.**]

[**From a later letter:**] I'm sure that by now you know that Judson Sapp died February 6 after a relatively brief but valiant fight against bone cancer. His knowledge of and enthusiasm for the mystery field will be missed. Even more will he be missed as a friend--a man whose warmth and openness made everyone feel at ease.

My thanks to John Reilly for his elucidations re **Twentieth**

Century Crime and Mystery Writers. I did not feel that the letter belabored the issue.

For Jiro Kimura: Judson Phillips (Hugh Pentecost) won the Nero Wolfe Award.

Great cover on 7:1. We're lucky to have Mr. Foster.

From Brad W. Foster, 4109 Pleasant Run, Irving, TX 75062:

Only glanced over the issue so far, I'm trying to reply to mail as soon as it comes in to keep it from building up again! Look forward to reading "Detection by Other Means," which at a look over sounds interesting. Ditto reading "Burlesques...," and—ah, hell, the whole thing looks good. I'm in the middle of **Titus Groan** right now, but this issue of TMF will be next in the stack beside the bed.[...]

My ego pushed me into looking with a bit more detail at the letters, now, though. I think Al Mosier should be allowed a life-time free sub for saying nice things about my cover! And Bob Adey can have half-a-year if you can figure out when to cut it off, for saying something nice too.

From Greg Goode, Hahnenstr. 27; B1, Zi. 221, 5030 Hurth-Efferen, WEST GERMANY:

The other day I was in Bonn, book hunting. Everything in Bonn looks quite rich, chic and well-to-do. I was almost too intimidated to enter a certain Antiquariat (antique book shop) because it shouted MONEY. But I did enter. Among the English language books, mostly paperbacks, were straight novels, classics, travel guides, etc. But among some cookbooks and an old edition of Descartes' **Meditations** I found something which surprised me: Gold Medal 400, Howard Rigsby's **Lucinda**! I certainly agree with Messrs. Shibuk and Crider. This odd, bittersweet combination of Erskine Caldwell, H. Rider Haggard, L. Frank Baum, and the Brothers Grimm (with a touch of Woolrich here and there) should not be missed by anyone.

Coincidental that there should be so many comments about William P. McGivern in 7:1. The same week I received it, the movie **Die Ratte** came to Cologne. The English translation is **The Rat**, and the credits list it as being based on the book by McGivern. **The Rat**?? But many times title "translations" have nothing to do with the original, so I asked the projectionist what the English title was: **Countdown in Manhattan**. No book by that title by McGivern that I know of. But the story was clearly an altered **Night of the Juggler**, and the film starred James Brolin and Cliff Gorman. According to the copyright date on the film, it was 1979, but reference books give 1975 as the date of the film by this title. Does anyone know how many films since 1975 were based on McGivern's books?

I must disagree with Linda Toole about Nevil Shute's inclusion in **TCC&MW**. For being one of the earlier of the Shute-H. Innes-Alistair MacLean school of man-against-natural-laws type thrillers, he is worthy of study in the sense John Reilly explained in 7:1.

Joe R. Christopher, Department of English, Tarleton State University, Stephenville, TX 76402:

Received 7:1 and so I'll renew. I had mixed feelings about vol.

6, and so I hadn't done anything. I liked some things in vol. 6 very much, such as Bleiler's essay on the Carr novel; but I found my limited tastes being satisfied by about one article per issue (although I read the issues cover to cover). It's my limits, not yours; there are just a lot of areas in mystery fiction which don't interest me greatly—spies, for one example.

But I suppose, when I find two interesting items in 7:1—"Bloody Balaclava" and Bargainnier on Tom Stoppard—I'd best go for another year.

By the way, I suspect Lachman is right when he says people either like Woolrich of they don't. I read a novella years ago—"Jane Brown's Body," I think it was, reprinted in The Magazine of Fantasy and Science Fiction—found it poorly written, and have never tried again. *sigh* My limits, I'm sure.

[I'm glad you reupped, Joe. I expect a great many TMFers share your reaction to each individual issue—that is, they find a thing or two in each issue which particularly appeals to them but seldom are ecstatic about the whole thing. That, I'm afraid, comes with the territory. There are two types of fan magazines in the mystery field today: specialist fanzines which focus narrowly on a small facet of the genre—The Dossier, Echoes, the ParkerPhile, The Bony Bulletin, The Not So Private Eye, etc.—and generalist fanzines such as The Poisoned Pen, TAD, and TMF, which try to be all things to all people. A necessary result of the generalist approach is that such magazines cannot please all readers all the time—or even, in all likelihood, all readers some of the time. The best we can shoot for is to please enough of the readers enough of the time to get them to renew each year, and I'm delighted to know that we've succeeded in your case, at least for volume 7.]

From Jim Goodrich, 61 Plains Rd., New Paltz, NY 12561:

Praise be, a change in the front cover design and new department heads. May I suggest that Brad do a cover inspired by **Spicy Detec**? Steve Lewis's "Mystery*File" departure is like losing a leg. I trust, too, that Steve will keep in touch via articles and letters. As compensation, we have Walter Albert's "Reel Murders," which I find to be **must** reading. How I envy him the opportunity to view the Melies films! It is very difficult to exist in '83 when Bob Sampson so lovingly describes the delights of Steve's magazine exchange in far away Charleston, West Virginia. Before I return to 1940, I better secure a lifeline to the present by renewing my **TMF** sub. Check enclosed. By the bye, would I be eligible to join the Popular Culture Association? That way we could meet elsewhere than in Beautiful Downtown Dayton, Ohio!

[Let's ask Jane Bakerman, one of several TMFers who belong to the PCA: Jane, is there any rule against lecherous librarians joining the Association?]

From Melinda Reynolds, Rt. 2, Box 93B, Corydon, KY 42406:

[Melinda submitted the following as an article, under the title "Women Mystery Writers: Thanks, But No Thanks...." I thought that, since the controversy had begun (and was likely to continue) in this column, I might as well run the article as a letter instead, so I made a few changes, and here it is.]

When asked—in a rather circuitous fashion, I admit—to give my opinions on a certain sector of mystery writers, I wasn't sure how to approach a potentially touchy subject without incurring the justifiable wrath of legions of readers. I am well aware that any subject will have its own group of fans and vociferous defenders; therefore, I usually adopt the following policy: "You can't please everyone, so please yourself." So, if anyone wishes to take umbrage, I'm sure Guy Townsend will be very happy to present opposing views.

I'll begin with Dorothy L. Sayers and her hero, Lord Peter Wimsey—who is her "hero" in every sense of the word; the lady dotes on him, an obvious detriment to the character she has created. To me, Lord Peter comes across as the personification of high-class, insipid indolence hiding behind the thin facade of a self-effacing "silly ass" caricature of the titled aristocrat. The books I managed to complete (**Clouds of Witness, Unnatural Death, Strong Poison,** and **Busman's Honeymoon**) all conveyed the same overall feeling for the Wimsey character: a prissy wimp in both mannerisms and speech, addicted to endless and insufferable prattle. I was hoping that Lord Peter, at some point, would eventually show a more mature and manly behavior, but then after reading about his outre family, I can at least understand why he turned out the way he did. I'm never really sure why he bothers to involve himself in solving mysteries: he's not a student of crime; it's not a hobby; he has no interest in the people involved, usually viewing each case as how it will personally affect him. He seems to be more of a nuisance than a help, as he is forever adopting a superior attitude of "being above it all." Lord Peter appears to be the other extreme to the "hard-boiled" detective genre (which I loathe); I much prefer the balance between the two detective types. As a light, mundane, romantic comedy of errors, Lord Peter and Dorothy L. Sayers is delightful reading; but as serious mystery, it falls flat.

Much has been said in favor of Ngaio Marsh's novels concerning Inspector/Superintendent Roderick Alleyn; however, after reading several of the novels (**Death in Ecstasy, Hand in Glove, Photo Finish, Grave Mistake,** and **Light Thickens**) I fail to see how her writing rates such praise. Alleyn is a very shallow character—plodding, methodical, and not very interesting. Most of her novels have a "padded" feel, as if she were attempting to fill up a required number of pages with whatever comes to mind. The plots are thin, somewhat contrived, and the stories are not fortunate enough to be sustained with good characterization.

P.D. James' writing is more in the vein of Journalism, with the inevitable descriptive paragraphs added to fill out the novel. Adam Dalgliesh is mediocre, as he (Like Alleyn, Grant, et al) goes through the expected police procedural motions to great and lengthly extent; but he at least has a good sense of humor about it all. James's books remind me of historical romance novels with history and/or geography lessons to expand the story with unnecessary and boring details. Such details that are needed can be better described in a few concise sentences. I read only two novels in the Dalgliesh series (**Black Tower** and **Death of an Expert Witness**) and was left with no desire to read the remaining titles.

Josephine Tey's novels are similar to those of James and Marsh, and my reaction to her writing is the same sense of apathy toward further reading; there is one addition—her character, Inspector Alan Grant, has an irritating habit of continually asking himself questions about whatever case he is working on. I read only two novels in this series: **Man in the Queue** and **A Shilling for Candles.**

Margery Allingham's "novels of suspense" fall far below that ambitious claim. Her detective, Albert Campion, is an uninspired (and uninspiring) bore, a one-dimensional character with little or no depth or feeling. Again, after reading three books, I had no desire to continue the series (**Tether's End, Allingham Casebook,** and **The Mind Readers**).

As to the noticeable absence of Agatha Christie—I have never been able to force myself to read beyond fifty or so pages of any of her novels. Her writing style and characterizations grate on my nerves. I cannot, for the life of me, see what it is that so fascinates and holds her multitude of readers. But the undeniable fact that she has hundreds of thousands of devotees is more or less an indication that either I am unable to pick up on whatever is attracting the other readers, or I have a "mental block" of some kind against her style of writing. I might note, also, that I haven't liked any of the movies based on her novels—although this may mean nothing, knowing Hollywood's propensity for taking liberties with novels.

Although written by different authors with varying styles, I have noted that all the novels [I have] mentioned [...] have the following similarities:

1) The characters range from bland and colorless to ridiculous, and all are unbelievable.

2) All employ a convoluted route to explain the simplest matters, supposedly for dramatic effect, but by the time the explanation is reached the reader's interest has waned.

3) The writers fail to generate any feeling or sense of involvement between the characters and the reader—I honestly didn't care who did it, or why, or how, and I had little or no interest in the main characters.

4) The novels are much too long, with unneeded, seemingly endless "descriptive" paragraphs or useless dialog—could have used strict editing and "tightening-up" to enhance the overall effect of the novel and to bring the denouement into sharper focus, producing a greater impact.

5) I experienced more negative reactions with the novels that positive feelings.

6) Novels by the various authors seemed to run together: I have never confused a Sherlock Holmes story with an Ellery Queen adventure, or a Rex Stout mystery with a Dick Francis novel.

The women writers not included in this [letter], i.e. Catherine Aird, Elizabeth Daly, Ruth Rendell, Mary Roberts Rinehart, and a few others, all failed to hold my interest past the first few paragraphs. So for now, when it comes to the lady authors and their mysterious works, I think I'll pass.

www.ingramcontent.com/pod-product-compliance
Lightning Source LLC
Chambersburg PA
CBHW031435040426
42444CB00006B/816